English
Listening and Speaking
for Academic Purposes

A Course Book
for Graduate Students

研究生
学术英语

视 听 说

总主编　陈新仁　黄　燕

主　编　杨奕枫　陈　萱

副主编　裴黎萍

编　者　杨奕枫　陈　萱

　　　　裴黎萍　程　欣

清華大學出版社

北 京

内 容 简 介

　　《研究生学术英语视听说》是"研究生学术英语实用教程"系列教材之一。本教材面向学生参与国际学术会议的现实需求，依据国际会议的流程进行内容编排，帮助学生掌握学术会议各个环节所需的语言策略和交流技巧。与同类教材相比，本教材围绕国际学术会议的重要环节进行理论讲解、技能训练与实践讨论，有针对性地锻炼学生在学术交流场景下聆听和分享学术成果的语言应用能力，更具系统性和操作性。

图书在版编目（CIP）数据

　　研究生学术英语视听说 / 陈新仁，黄燕总主编；杨奕枫，陈萱主编. —北京：清华大学出版社，2022.6 (2025.7重印)
　　ISBN 978-7-302-60915-5

　　I. ①研…　Ⅱ. ①陈…　②黄…　③杨…　④陈…　Ⅲ. ①英语—听说教学—研究生—教材　Ⅳ. ① H319.9

　　中国版本图书馆 CIP 数据核字（2022）第 088666 号

责任编辑：刘细珍
封面设计：李尘工作室
责任校对：王凤芝
责任印制：杨　艳

出版发行：清华大学出版社
　　　　　网　　　址：https://www.tup.com.cn, https://www.wqxuetang.com
　　　　　地　　　址：北京清华大学学研大厦 A 座　　邮　　编：100084
　　　　　社 总 机：010-83470000　　　　　　　邮　　购：010-62786544
　　　　　投稿与读者服务：010-62776969, c-service@tup.tsinghua.edu.cn
　　　　　质量反馈：010-62772015, zhiliang@tup.tsinghua.edu.cn
印 装 者：三河市君旺印务有限公司
经　　销：全国新华书店
开　　本：185mm×260mm　　　　**印　张：**9.75　　　　**字　数：**191 千字
版　　次：2022 年 6 月第 1 版　　　　　　　　　　**印　次：**2025 年 7 月第 3 次印刷
定　　价：56.00 元

产品编号：095238-02

总　序

研究生教育肩负着国家高层次人才培养和创新创造的重要使命，是国家发展、社会进步的重要基石。研究生英语课程对于持续提高研究生的人文素养和专业能力，培养学生的家国情怀和创新精神，引导学生坚定文化自信、学术自信，成为有理想、有国际学术视野的高层次、创新性人才，从而更好地服务于国家的发展战略，都具有不可替代的重要作用。

为贯彻落实教育部印发的《高等学校课程思政建设指导纲要》，彰显立德树人根本宗旨，培养研究生的学术英语能力和跨文化交流能力，深入推进新时代研究生培养国际化，我们秉持"以学生学习为中心"的教育学理念，结合我国研究生英语学习实际需求和教学现状，策划编写了本套"研究生学术英语实用教程"系列教材，由《研究生学术英语阅读：理工类》《研究生学术英语阅读：人文类》《研究生学术英语写作：理工类》《研究生学术英语写作：人文类》《研究生学术英语视听说》共五册教材构成。

本套教材的编写原则与思路如下：

一、以立德树人为总目标，秉承以学生发展为中心、以学生学习为中心的理念，两个中心相辅相成，互为支撑。以学生发展为中心体现在将思政教育有机融入教材设计中，内容选择与问题设计体现中国学术贡献、学术诚信、文化自信、科学素养等思政元素。以学生学习为中心体现在内容设计围绕真实的学术活动展开，满足学生用英语进行专业学习、开展国际学术交流的现实需要。

二、着眼于跨文化学术交际，体现国际化人才培养的定位。本套教材将学术交流置于跨文化语境之中，注重培养学生的国际视野和跨文化学术交际意识，提升跨文化沟通中所需的学术交流能力和思辨能力。一方面，各分册的选材都能兼顾中外学者、中英文学术语篇，提供比较分析的机会。另一方面，各分册所选语料都蕴含具体的学术体裁知识，为学生习得跨文化学术交流所需的各种学术英语知识提供必要的支持。

三、本着"在用中学"的编写理念，着力于学生多元能力培养。新时代深化研究生培养改革，必须着力增强研究生实践能力、创新能力等多元能力的培养。本套教材强调能力培养至上而非知识传授至上。各分册采用"以项目为导向"的学术英语教学方法，注重实际学术活动的参与和体验，以输入驱动输出，将听、说、读、写、译五项语言技能有机融合，强调综合语言应用能力、合作学习、自主学习能力的培养，激励学生通过讨论及修改反例等练习形式提升批判性思辨能力。

四、体现学术共性与学科差异。基于大类学科（如理工类、人文类）的特点，设计各分册，每个分册选材真实地道，来源多样，内涵丰富。同一单元涵盖多门学科，体现大学科特色，以支撑高校主流学科国际化人才的培养。

五、体现信息技术支撑。为实现教材编写目标，培养学生的自主学习能力，本套教材在各分册中都设计了让学生利用互联网自主查找文献或相关资源的教学活动。另外，全套教材采用线上与线下相结合的方式提供课堂教学资源和拓展学习资源。

本着上述编写原则和思路，"研究生学术英语实用教程"系列教材形成以下鲜明特色：

- **育人性。**各分册每个单元都有课程思政的元素，全套教材强调学术诚信和科学素养，力求将育人寓于学术英语知识传授和多元能力培养之中。

- **实用性。**全套教材所选语料来源于真实学术活动，内容设计切实贴近学生实际阅读、写作、听说需求，为其英语学习提供全面、切实、有效的指导。

- **针对性。**全套教材面向国内非英语专业研究生，在整个编写过程中，以学生为中心，关注他们的实际需求，聚焦他们在学习过程中的重难点，力求合理把握教学内容的难度，为学生提供丰富的、可学可用的语料。

- **可操作性。**全套教材练习形式多样，采用结对练习、小组讨论等形式凸显互动性和合作性，强调获得感。各分册均由八个单元构成，满足 16 个标准课堂学时的教学需要，服务课堂操作。

作为体现学术共性与学科差异的学术英语系列教材，本套教材可以满足不同院校、不同学科研究生英语教学需要。我们诚挚欢迎广大英语教师和各位学生在使用本套教材的过程中，能以各种方式提供反馈意见和建议，以便我们不断完善，打造一套启智润心、增知强能的系列精品教材！

陈新仁、黄燕
2022 年 4 月

前 言

　　《研究生学术英语视听说》是"研究生学术英语实用教程"系列教材之一。在具体呈现整套教材立德树人的总体编写理念、思路与特色的基础上，本册教材旨在满足我国研究生参与各种形式的国际学术口语交流的现实需要，聚力训练学生的学术英语听力和口语表达能力，特别是在国际学术会议和其他学术研讨场合用英语进行演讲、宣读论文、即席答辩、交谈讨论等方面的实际能力。

本册特色

- **国际学术会议全流程覆盖。**本教材各单元内容编排以国际学术会议的一般流程为依据，指导学生掌握学术会议各个环节所需的语言策略和交流技巧，提升学生参与国际会议的信心与能力。

- **英语听说技能训练全方位融合。**本教材针对学生在研究生阶段提升学术英语交流能力的需求，将理论讲解、单项技能训练、综合技能训练和交流任务训练深度结合，帮助学生全面提升学术交流场景下的语言应用能力。

教材构成

　　本教材以学术交流为主线，根据国际会议的流程进行内容编排。全书共分为八个单元，每个单元针对一个会议环节展开，主题依次为自我介绍、研究介绍、学术报告、回答问题、参与专场讨论、提问、主持会议以及学术会议期间的社交。

　　每个单元包括八个部分。第一部分为内容概览，旨在帮助学生了解教学目标，并快速抓取单元内容。第二部分是听说技能介绍，讲解本单元听说活动相关的知识点和技能，帮助学生深入了解单元内容。第三部分是学术口语表达常用句型，给学生提供在实际场景中可以运用的一些口语表达的句型，方便学生记忆、操练，为学生进行任务训练做准备。第四部分是听力专项训练，采用多样的练习形式（补全信息、填空、正误判断、选择题、简答题等），着重训练学生理解大意、抓住细节、归纳总结的听力技能；材料难度上遵循循序渐进的原则，内容包括知识点和技能介绍的微课视频以及真实学术场景的音频和视频节选。第五部分是口语专项训练，是前面部分的自然延伸和发展；该部分旨在结合知识点和技能，使用常用句型表达，指导学生进行口语操练。第六部分是听说综合任务，采用角色扮演、对话、讨论、汇报等不同形式的活动，针对各项听力和口语专项技能进行综合训练。第七部分是课外练习，供学生自主学习，帮助学生检查听力、口语学习效果。第八部分是团队项目，根据单元内容，模拟国际会议中的一个流程，让学生以团队为单位完成一项综合性口语任务。

教学建议

本教材每个单元的八个部分组成一个有机的整体。其中第七部分供学生课外自主学习和训练。由于该部分所使用的音视频材料比其他部分略长，而且多半结合了听力和口语任务，教师可以布置为家庭作业，课堂上只需做适当检查，或要求学生课后录制成视频与全班分享。单元的其他部分由教师当堂讲授和操练。建议每四个课时完成一个单元。教师可根据课堂时间安排等具体情况灵活处理各部分内容。

编写分工

本教材由杨奕枫、陈萱担任主编，裴黎萍担任副主编。各单元分工情况如下：杨奕枫，第三、四单元；陈萱，第一、八单元；程欣，第二、七单元；裴黎萍，第五、六单元。陈新仁教授和黄燕教授审阅全部材料和书稿，并负责审改、润色文稿。

本教材为总主编陈新仁教授主持的南京大学研究生"三个一百"优质课程建设项目"博士生英语口语"的部分成果。

由于编者水平有限、编写时间仓促，书中难免有疏漏和错误之处，敬请广大同仁和英语学习者不吝批评指正。

编 者
2022 年 5 月

Contents

Unit 1

Introducing Your Academic Self

Part I
Introducing the Unit

Introducing yourself to others has become a very common activity in daily life. You may have to do it when you meet new people or when you come to a new place. It is also quite necessary in academic settings. Students or novice researchers alike need to give a self-introduction when they attend a conference or when they sit at their own oral defense meeting. They can hardly avoid introducing themselves when they socialize with others in academic settings.

In this unit, we are going to present the basics about giving a self-introduction, including the basic structure, general principles and common variations at academic events. You will listen to some examples of self-introduction, analyze them, and then practice creating your own version.

Part II
Learning about the Activity

A self-introduction should cover the essential details that others need to know about you, for example, your name, university or affiliation, major or specialization, and other key facts that will help you make a positive impression on those you are speaking to. In a sense, a self-introduction can make or break the first impression.

→ Structure

The basic structure of a self-introduction usually consists of a starter, a description of your academic self and a smooth transition to the next part.

❶   A starter (optional)

Instead of beginning your self-introduction right away with your name and title, you can opt for a starter. It can be a fact, a group of statistics, a recent experience, or a question to arouse the curiosity of your audience. Whatever your choice, it should relate to the theme of your presentation and meanwhile grab the attention of your audience.

❷   A description of your academic self

When describing yourself, you need to state your name clearly and emphatically. Then you can introduce your job title / experience, or your educational degree and certification level. When you give an overview of your background, your achievements or contributions, keep it in mind that your purpose is to communicate your expertise to the audience so as to gain trust and reliability. Therefore the information you include should be pertinent to the purpose.

❸   A smooth transition to the next part

To avoid abruptness, you can add a smooth transition to the next part of your talk. For a presentation, you can conclude your self-introduction with a lead-in to what you plan to discuss. A self-introduction to a new acquaintance at a conference can end with a call for further correspondence.

→ Principles

When preparing your self-introduction, remember the following five principles, namely, brevity, relevancy, truthfulness, confidence and humor. They will help you in unexpected ways.

❶ Brevity

Keep your introduction short. A terse introduction is generally powerful. Go straight to the point. Focus on your most important achievements. Show your expertise. All these will make your introduction impressive and memorable.

❷ Relevancy

A good introduction must be tailored to your purpose. You need to include details most relevant to the person you're speaking to. If you are giving a conference presentation, offer information that supports your authority in the area you are speaking on. If you are at your oral defense or project report, mention the efforts you have exerted and the preparation you have made for your thesis or project.

Ensure that the information you include in your introduction is related to your speech. Don't go off course. The extra details can be left on a handout or PPT slide if you think they are truly interesting and relevant.

❸ Truthfulness

Since you are introducing yourself, be as truthful as possible. You do not need to brag about your achievements or contributions to demonstrate your expertise, because honesty is the best policy.

❹ Confidence

It is equally important for you to demonstrate the image of a confident Chinese research student or scholar. Your confidence lies in your rigorous research methods, your years of hard work, and a truthful way of reporting results. You have every reason to be confident in yourself. However, be aware not to overdo it so that you sound arrogant.

❺ Humor

A touch of humor can create an instant connection between you and your audience. It can also help put both of you at ease. You can start by making fun of yourself or exaggerating your own experiences in a humorous way. But make sure that any jokes or ironies you use are natural and appropriate for the context in which you are speaking. You can start cultivating your sense of humor from now on, and do not force it into your self-introduction if you are not ready.

Apart from these general principles, a good self-introduction requires the speaker to know the audience, know their familiarity with the topic, their needs and their cultural background. The speaker also needs to pay attention to his/her own body language, including eye-contact with the audience, posture and other non-verbal communication skills. All these will help the speaker to achieve success in the presentation.

Part III
Learning Useful Expressions

➜ At a conference presentation

- Today, I'm going to share a story of how someone with zero marketing skills and training made it to the top through...in just 6 months.

- If you're passionate about..., this is for you. Stay tuned till the end for better insights.

- Hi, my name is...I've got...years' worth of experience in helping business owners boost their sales. I enjoy teaching people how to connect with the right audience at the right time. With my experience in this field, I've helped several entrepreneurs map out proven strategies in getting massive sales. I'm looking forward to working with you all.

- Today's gathering reminded me of a recent burning at...Many people blamed the occupant for the incident. But my understanding of climate gives me another insight into the issue...My name is...I work with...

- Would you believe if I told you that you could reach 15k+ people on LinkedIn in just 30 days? No? Stick around for the next...minutes as I'm going to teach you all about it so you can get started as a rookie with zero connections.

- Hi everyone! I'm XYZ—a Linked Growth Hacker. I've been helping businesses grow and build a strong personal brand for five years now. If you're wondering how to generate leads on LinkedIn, take note of the pointers I'll be sharing with you today.

→ At an oral defense

- Good morning, dear professors and my fellow classmates. I am...Thank you for attending my oral thesis defense!

- I've been teaching at...for...years. Throughout these years, I've always been puzzled by a problem: ...Now after years of research, I've finally found a solution. Please allow me to present it to you.

- I've been studying...for...years. During this time, I've developed an interest in...In the past...years, my supervisor has helped me to narrow it down to...Today I'm going to explain to you...

- I had...years of work experience before entering this graduate program. The topic I chose to focus on in my thesis combines my personal interest with the hottest topic in the field.

- The topic of my thesis has nothing to do with my past experience but everything to do with...

Part IV
Practicing Listening

Task 1

Watch an excerpt from the TED talk "The Single Biggest Reason Why Start-ups Succeed" by Bill Gross and complete the following exercises.

1. **Watch the video ONCE and fill each blank with NO MORE THAN FOUR words.**

I'm really excited to share with you some findings that really surprise me about what makes companies succeed the most, (1) _____ the most for start-up success.

I believe that the start-up organization is one of the greatest forms to make the world a better place. If you take a group of people with the right equity (2) _____ and organize them in a start-up, you can (3) _____ in a way never before possible. You get them to achieve unbelievable things.

But if the start-up organization is so great, why do so many fail? That's what I wanted to find out. I wanted to find out (4) _____ most for start-up success.

And I wanted to try to be (5) _____ about it, avoid some of my (6) _____ and maybe (7) _____ I have from so many companies I've seen over the years.

I wanted to know this because (8) _____ since I was 12 years old when I sold candy at the bus stop in junior high school, to high school, when I made (9) _____, to college, when I made loudspeakers. And when I graduated from college, I started software companies. And 20 years ago, I started Idealab, and in the last 20 years, we started more than 100 companies, many successes, and many big failures. We learned a lot from those failures.

So I (10) _____ what factors accounted the most for company success and failure.

2.   **Watch again and answer the following questions.**

   1) What is the structure of this introduction?

   _____

   _____

   _____

   2) How did the speaker connect his starter with his personal history?

   _____

   _____

   _____

   3) Why did the speaker mention his years of experience in this field?

   _____

   _____

   _____

   4) Can you guess what kind of position the speaker held in his field without checking the Internet? If you still don't know this person, check about the answer on the Internet. Now can you tell why he didn't give his self-introduction right at the beginning?

   _____

   _____

   _____

Task 2

Watch an excerpt from the mini-lecture "How to Use Humor in a Speech Opening" by Alex Lyon and complete the following exercises. Then compare the answers in pairs.

1.   **Watch the video ONCE and fill each blank with NO MORE THAN THREE words.**

   Other professional-level speakers say: You should start your presentation

   (1) _____.

   Alex acknowledges that attention-grabber is (2) _____.

   He (3) _____ telling a set-up punchline style joke, the kind that a stand-up comic would tell.

He is 100% in favor of (4) _____ in a presentation.

He can give you a straight-ahead way to (5) _____ without the big risk of a punchline style joke.

2. **Watch the video again and answer the following questions.**

1) What is the structure of this introduction part of Alex's speech?

_____

_____

_____

2) How many sentences did Alex use to describe himself? What is the purpose of these sentences?

_____

_____

_____

3. **Write down the expressions Alex used to transit his opening to the main talk.**

_____

_____

_____

 ## Task 3

Watch the beginning part of the lecture "The Perfect Defense: The Oral Defense of a Dissertation" by Dr. Valerie Balester and choose the TWO right answers to each of the following questions.

1. **Why did Dr. Balester mention her position and her experience of attending more than 60 defenses?**

    A. To show her expertise on this topic.

    B. To illustrate her knowledge about dissertation defense.

    C. To demonstrate her familiarity about the structure of dissertation defense.

2. **How did she make transition from her self-introduction to the essence of her lecture?**

    A. By giving concrete details about what happens in a defense meeting.

    B. By asking the audience relevant questions.

    C. By answering the questions she raised to the audience.

Part V
Practicing Speaking

Task 1

Suppose you are going to give an oral defense of your thesis in a few days. Prepare a brief self-introduction for your oral defense meeting and present it to your classmates. Include your personal information and your reasons to choose the research topic.

Task 2

Suppose you have just finished writing a research article. Your supervisor asks you to present it at an upcoming international conference. Write a self-introduction for your presentation and present it to the whole class.

Task 3

Watch a self-introduction given by Snehal Awate, an Assistant Professor at the Indian School of Business, and figure out what you can learn from her self-introduction. Work in pairs and take turns to introduce yourself. Take some notes while listening and discuss with your partner how to improve your performance.

Task 4

Work in groups. Go to the Internet and find the beginning part of a presentation at a recent academic conference or an oral defense meeting. Make sure it contains the speaker's self-introduction. Use the following checklist to assess this introduction. Discuss with your group members and vote for the best example in your group.

Assessment Checklist

Aspects for you to consider	Yes	No
Does the speaker include a relevant and interesting starter?		
Does the speaker demonstrate his/her expertise in the field through the self-introduction?		
Does the speaker include a smooth transition to the next part?		
Is the self-introduction brief?		

(Continued)

Aspects for you to consider	Yes	No
Is the information included in the self-introduction relevant to the speech?		
Does it demonstrate the speaker's self-confidence without any complacence?		
Does the self-introduction have a touch of humor?		

Part VI
Performing the Activity

Situation 1

The whole class will attend a seminar. Each student will take turns to give a self-introduction in groups, and observe carefully the other group members' performance. At the end of the activity, vote for the best presenters and observe their performance.

Step 1: Divide the whole class into five to six groups.

Step 2: Each student will take turns to give a self-introduction in the group.

Step 3: Vote for the best presenter in each group.

Step 4: The best presenters will demonstrate in front of the whole class.

Situation 2

Write a self-introduction for a workshop on international publications. You should include your personal information, research interest, target international journals and the reasons for choosing them. Then work in a group of three. Take turns to present your self-introduction to your partners and ask for feedback about your strengths and weaknesses.

Step 1: Write a self-introduction for the workshop. Make sure to include your personal information, research interest, your target international journals and reasons for your choice.

Step 2: Divide the whole class into groups of three.

Step 3: Present your self-introduction to the group.

Step 4: Keep notes of the strengths and weaknesses of your partners' presentations.

Step 5: Give feedback to one another on how to improve the performance.

📖 Exercises

 Task 1

Watch the complete mini-lecture "How to Use Humor in a Speech Opening" by Alex Lyon and finish the following exercises.

1. **Watch the video ONCE and take down notes with the form. Then watch again to check your answers.**

    ### Three Easy Ways to Add Humor and Grab Attention

_____	What you are doing is drawing others' attention to what that other person said, and it takes _____ _____. Both you and your audience focus on that little line, and if it bombs, and that's not really on you.
_____	If you add a certain _____ to the people in your story, your story become humorous _____ _____.
_____	For example, a _____, a _____. It is a _____ way.
Restatement of his main idea:	100% against _____, and 100% in favor of _____.

2. **Work in pairs. Retell the three ways to add humor and grab attention to each other without referring back to the notes. Then tell each other which way you think is the easiest and why.**

3. **Search the Internet to find some jokes or funny pictures related to one of the topics you are going to present at an upcoming conference.**

Task 2

Watch the self-introduction by Dr. Becky da Cruz at Armstrong State University and complete the exercises.

1. **Watch the video ONCE and complete the details of the following notes.**

Her _____ background	Bachelor of Arts in _____; A degree in _____; A PhD in Human Services with a specialization in _____.
Her _____ experience	Began teaching _____ in 1996, full time in 1998. Began teaching at Armstrong in 2003. Started teaching _____ in 2001. Worked in the Prosecutor's office and in the criminal field. Practiced law on the civil side.
Her _____ in teaching this course	To make it an _____ learning process in order to _____ student interest in the subjective matter.
_____ will she achieve this	She does this by _____ students to a variety of learning modalities, e.g., reading, writing, videos, debates, and applied exercises. The _____ is to immerse the students into the material to see how it _____ their lives.
Who might be interested in the course	Students who like studying abroad; Students interested in _____: It is the best way to prepare for the rigorous law school.
Her _____ as a teacher	She will help the students _____ both in this course and as they move through their time here in Armstrong.
Her _____	Her email, telephone, office, and the best time to reach her.

2. **Apart from helping others to know her, what could be the other purpose for Dr. da Cruz to include these details about herself and her course?**

_____

_____

_____

3. If you are to open a course in your field, how will you introduce yourself?

    _____

    _____

    _____

Task 3

Watch the beginning of a PhD dissertation defense by Faizan Shafique from Michigan State University and answer the following questions.

1. What is the structure of the beginning of Dr. Shafique's defense?

    _____

    _____

    _____

2. Why did he include a modified group picture of his committee members and himself in his acknowledgement?

    _____

    _____

    _____

3. What did he include in his self-introduction? What was his focus and why?

    _____

    _____

    _____

Task 4

Sometimes you need to introduce yourself when you mingle with other scholars at a conference or in some other academic or non-academic settings. Should you do it formally or informally? What are the differences in content and in language? Watch a mini-lecture entitled "Introduce Yourself in English with Ease" and then answer the following questions.

1. What decides whether you should choose a formal style or an informal one when doing a self-introduction?

    _____

_____

_____

2. Create two versions of self-introduction, a formal one and an informal one.

_____

_____

_____

_____

_____

_____

3. Rehearse your self-introductions to your roommates and ask them for suggestions. After you have done the revision, present the self-introductions to the whole class.

Task 5

When you are applying for a new job in the research field, you sometimes need to introduce your personal details. Watch the video of Ting Hu, a Chinese scholar, and complete the following exercises.

1. Watch the video ONCE and take notes of the personal details the scholar has covered in her answer to the questions.

_____

_____

_____

2. Why do you think the school asks about her standard of choosing a graduate student? What are her standards?

_____

_____

_____

3. Watch the video again and take notes of all the questions asked in this video. Meanwhile, observe carefully the way this scholar answers them. Practice answering these questions with some adaptation to your own research field.

_____

_____

_____

📖 Project

Suppose you are invited to give a presentation at an international conference. You are requested to submit a bio-note of yourself in addition to your title and abstract. Work in a group of three. Look for some samples of bio-notes, discuss how they are written, and help each other work out their own bio-notes. Then choose the best one to present in class.

Unit 2

Introducing Your Research

Part I
Introducing the Unit

How do you talk to people about your research? It is a question worth spending time thinking about because you cannot avoid it whether attending graduate school interviews, networking at academic conferences, attracting funding and collaboration, or simply explaining to your friends and family what you are working on. On different occasions, you might have to introduce your research in different ways, since you do not want to bore your audience or confuse them.

This unit will focus on introducing your research in a general way, such as your general research interest, research experience and the institutes or teams you work in. We will leave the presentation of a specific research project to the next unit. Hopefully, this unit will give you some ideas on how to talk about your research work in a more appealing way.

Part II
Learning about the Activity

With years of devotion to research, you might find it difficult to introduce your research in just a few minutes. But talking about your research is different from writing a research paper. Whoever you are talking to, the purpose is to catch listeners' attention, and to engage them so that they want to learn more about your research. Therefore, the trick is to give listeners a bigger picture, and try to relate your research to them. Now, let's have a look at the strategies you can use to take others into your research world.

❶ Consider your audience

Be aware that when you talk about your research, the audience can be anyone, from the specialists in your field to the general public. You need to tailor the content to your audience. Otherwise, they may not understand what you say; as a result, they may not know why you put so much effort in your research, or why they would want to work with you or fund you in the future. It is important that you perform early audience analysis, and gauge the level of knowledge and expectations of your audience.

For example, you need to choose the language appropriate to your audience. If you are talking to specialists in the same field as you, you do not need to get rid of the technical terms, and you probably need to give more details about the work you have done. If you are talking to people who specialize in a related field, you probably do not need to avoid jargon, but you will need to elaborate on the significance and benefits of your research. To a layperson, however, it is important to use plain language, and focus more on why you are doing it rather than what it is.

❷ Focus on shared interest

The first thing in building a talk is to find out your core message. No matter how well you conduct your research, it is naive to assume that everyone is equally intrigued by your research. The right focus varies with your audience. As mentioned above, you need to consider who your audience are, what they have already known, and what they are interested in. Once you start to explore the common ground, and think about which aspect of your research is relevant to your audience or conversational partners, the chances to trigger their interest will greatly increase.

For example, suppose you study positive emotions, such as feelings of joy, wonder, and compassion, and your findings have clinical implications because they can inform theories about mental illness as well as interventions that may help people manage their emotions. If you talk with people from psychology department, you can focus on how your work can test psychological theories. If you speak to a group of practitioners, you need to focus on how your research can help patients. If you talk to a layperson, perhaps you can focus on what motivated you, and how your findings can help people with their emotions.

❸ Explain "why", not "what"

One mistake many people make when talking about their research is to start with "what" their research is and how they conduct it. But when you only have a few minutes, there is no way to explain in detail about your research. To catch listeners' attention, you need to first tell them why you are conducting your research. Put your research in a broader context, and start with what motivates you and what problems your research contributes to solve. It may be something that has interested you from childhood, or it could cure a disease, or help understand a phenomenon. Whatever it is, your explanation of "why" will provide a basis on which your listeners can then build their understanding.

❹ Personalize your research

By personalizing your research, you and your research are connected. This can often make a deeper impression on your listeners. You can share your research stories by telling the audience how you end up doing this research, how your research interests have developed, where you have done the research, etc. You can also introduce the university, institution, or research team you are in, since doing research is often team work. The achievement of your team can often help explain the significance of your work.

Part III
Learning Useful Expressions

➜ Talking about your research interest

- For me, ...is an interesting area because... / I'm interested in... / I'm super into...

- ...motivated me to conduct research.

- I'm passionate about... / I enjoy... / I fell in love with...

- My particular specialism is in...I research how...

- I particularly focus on... / look at... / study...

- Mostly I work on...

➜ Talking about your affiliation

- I'm at...Institute/University, and I'm working on a research program which focuses on...

- I'm a student at...University studying...

- Doing a PhD in...is really helpful, because...is well recognized.

- My laboratory focuses primarily on...

- Our lab aims to...

- We have superb research environment and an innovation-encouraging tradition.

- Our research team is divided into...groups, focusing on different directions.

- We do research related to...

Part IV
Practicing Listening

Task 1

This video tells you how to talk about your research to others. Watch the video TWICE, and answer the questions.

1. **What is an elevator pitch?**

    _____

    _____

    _____

2. **What are the things to consider as you plan your pitch?**

    _____

    _____

    _____

3. **What are the potential pitfalls?**

    _____

    _____

    _____

4. **What are the two important things to consider as you finalize your research story?**

    _____

    _____

    _____

Task 2

In this video, Ingomar Krohn describes his PhD study at WBS.

1. **Watch the video ONCE, and answer the following questions.**

    1) What research area is Ingomar Krohn interested in? Why?

    _____

_____

_____

2) What is Ingomar Krohn's plan after his PhD?

_____

_____

_____

2. **Watch the video again, and fill in each blank with NO MORE THAN TWO words.**

WBS is well recognized.	Once you drop the name WBS, especially in finance, people know what you are talking about, and they associate that with great _____.
PhD modules in the area of economics.	You're covering macroeconomics, econometrics, and _____, as well as finance-related topics such as _____, asset pricing, or market microstructure.
Benefits of the PhD community in WBS.	It's a great opportunity to share your ideas, to discuss your research topic, and to get _____ and new ideas from research fellows as well, because they're usually in the same situation as you are. You share the same _____ and _____.

Task 3

The video titled "A Passion for Research, a Passion for Life" introduces Christine Metz, PhD, who has dedicated her life to finding new ways to improve the lives of others.

1. **Watch the video ONCE, and answer the following questions.**
    1) Who is the speaker and what institute does she work for?

    _____

    _____

    2) What motivated Dr. Metz to do research?

    _____

    _____

3) According to Dr. Metz, what is the fun aspect of science, and what is the ultimate goal?

_____

_____

2. **Watch the video again, and fill in each blank with NO MORE THAN FOUR words.**

We facilitate (1) _____ research at Feinstein. It has an impact on better understanding and (2) _____. My laboratory focused primarily on conditions of (3) _____, and that means both moms' outcomes, in the short term or in the long term, and how it affects the (4) _____.

Part V
Practicing Speaking

Task 1

Watch a video clip in which Professor Helen Abbott (Department of Modern Languages) discusses her current research at the University of Birmingham. Then retell her research interest.

Task 2

Work in pairs, and describe to each other your current research interest.

Task 3

What motivated you to do research? What types of research have you done? Have you been interested in one research area all along or changed your research direction? Work in pairs, and share your research stories and experience with each other.

Task 4

Work in pairs or groups. Tell your partners why you are pursuing the degree at the current university/institute/lab.

Part VI
Performing the Activity

Situation 1

Work in pairs. Suppose you were high school classmates. You meet each other at a high school reunion party, and are asked by your former high school classmate what your work/ study is about. Introduce your research to him/her.

Step 1: Each student finds a partner to work with.

Step 2: Imagine that you do not know much about each other's work. Introduce your research to your partner, and give responses while listening.

Step 3: (Optional) Change partners, and form new pairs.

Step 4: (Optional) Tell your new partner what you hear from your first partner.

Situation 2

Suppose you are attending an international conference. At the coffee break, you introduce yourself and your affiliation to other attendees. In your introduction to your affiliation, you can include its scale, major research areas, teams, achievements, and ongoing projects. Present your description to your partners, and take questions, comments, or suggestions from the audience if possible.

Step 1: Divide the class into groups of four.

Step 2: Introduce yourself and your affiliation to others in the group.

Step 3: While listening, ask questions when you feel confused or curious.

Exercises

Task 1

In this video, Tiffany introduces her research internships.

1. Watch the video ONCE, and write down the two reasons given by Tiffany why students should do research in college.

   _____

   _____

2. Tiffany has been to many countries and regions over the world and had quite a few research internships. Match the places with her research areas.
   1) Hawaii   a) marine science
   2) China   b) ancient agriculture
   3) Monterey   c) artificial intelligence

3. Watch the video again, and fill in the blanks with the information you hear.

In a marine science lab	I used _____ to analyze _____ _____ in marine protected areas. Marine protected areas are _____. The research I did that summer ended up _____ _____ and will eventually help inform policy on _____ _____. So the work I did that one summer as a college student will help _____ _____.
In a biopsychology lab	We were studying how _____ _____. This connected the two fields that I was interested in, _____ and _____. This was my first research experience, and I learned that I really liked research and wanted to continue doing it. I also realized that I wanted to do something a little more _____. This finding eventually helped me decide on majoring in _____.

4.　Are there other reasons for doing research? Discuss with your partner, and illustrate your views with your own experience.

Task 2

In this video, Simon Clark describes how he chose his research field.

1.　Watch the video TWICE, and complete the details in the notes.

When he was a kid	He was super interested in _____, specifically _____. He was super into _____. He was aware of the issues of _____ and _____. He was determined to do something related to that.
When he went to school	He realized that the cool stuff was in _____. He decided to dedicate himself to the big hope for the future —_____.
When he got to university	He lost interest in the area of _____. He fell in love with the area of _____ _____. He found his focus again because it connected him back to _____, back to _____. This subject combines two things he was really interested in, _____ & the real world and the biosphere.

2.　Discuss with your partner on the message you get from Simon Clark's experience in finding the research interest.

Task 3

Here's an excerpt from a TED talk given by Professor Allen Chan on how he began to pursue a career in scientific research.

1.　Watch the video ONCE, and choose the right answers to the following questions.
　　1)　Why did Professor Chan go back to school to study a PhD?
　　　　A. A PhD program would train him to be a better doctor.
　　　　B. A PhD degree would help him find a better-paid job.
　　　　C. He was inspired by Professor Dennis Lowe's discovery.
　　　　D. He made a discovery which was considered as a conceptual breakthrough.

2) Which of the following statements is TRUE about the discovery?

    A. The baby's DNA can be found in the blood circulation of the pregnant woman.

    B. The pregnant woman can develop some antibody to attack the baby.

    C. The blood circulation of the baby and the pregnant woman is completely separated.

    D. The disease of the pregnant woman can infect the baby by blood circulation.

2. **Watch the video again, and fill in the blanks in the following paragraph which explains the clinical benefits brought by this discovery.**

We can develop new diagnostic methods to do (1) _____ , just by looking at the blood plasma of the (2) _____ . So conventionally, if we want to do prenatal testing, we need to put a (3) _____ of this long into the uterus of the pregnant woman to get some fetal materials. You can imagine how (4) _____ this process would be, and also it carries (5) _____ . So if we can use the mother's blood to do all the testing and (6) _____ from the mother's blood, it would be fantastic.

3. **As presented above, the benefits of the research were explained. When introducing our research to the general public, it is often more effective to start with why to do it than what it is or how to do it. Work with your partner, and tell each other the significance of the research you have been engaged in.**

Task 4

Your PhD interview will be an important part of your postgraduate research application. This is your chance to meet your prospective department, talk about your research interest and experience, and show your potential as an academic researcher. This video gives suggested answers to some of the possible PhD interview questions.

1. **Watch the video ONCE, and take notes on the advice given by the speaker.**

Questions	Advice
1) Could you please tell us about yourself?	✓ Show your _____ . ✓ Link to your _____ side. ✓ Talk about your background.

(Continued)

Questions	Advice
2) _____ _____	✓ Say that you _____ this topic. ✓ Say that you want to _____ . ✓ Say that you are _____ .
3) _____ _____	✓ Talk about what that lab can offer and the other groups might not have. ✓ Talk about what that lab has _____ , which aligns with what you are interested in. ✓ Talk about what _____ and _____ that lab has.
4) _____ _____	✓ Talk about what _____ you've done. ✓ Talk about what you can bring to that lab, e.g. some _____ , ability to do some coding, to use a particular _____ or a particular _____ . ✓ Talk about your _____ for that particular research project. ✓ Talk about any grades that are _____ _____ . ✓ Talk about any _____ for being the top. ✓ Say that you're _____ .

2. **Watch the video again and decide whether the following statements about the woman are true (T) or false (F).**

1) She grew up in London.   (   )

2) She studied in University College London.   (   )

3) She's been passionate about understanding cancer.   (   )

4) In graduate school, she fell in love with the topic of cell biology.   (   )

5) She enjoyed a research placement in a lab in her undergraduate years. (   )

6) She went to pursue a PhD because she enjoyed being in a lab working with other people towards a particular goal.   (   )

7) She has published some papers.   (   )

8) She achieved an award for being the top 5% in the university.   (   )

3. **Have a try and practice answering these interview questions. Then work in pairs, and take turns to interview each other.**

Task 5

As a strong promoter of China's technological innovations, Tsinghua's Institute of Artificial Intelligence has always been a beacon of cutting-edge research and innovation. This video introduces the eight research teams of the institute.

1. **Watch the video, and complete the notes on the research focus of each of the eight teams.**

Natural Language Processing	Teach computers to _____, speak and communicate with people. Make AI understand _____, and develop AI poet to write _____.
Natural Language Generation, Dialogue Systems	Work on text generation where AI can _____ _____.
AI Music, Computational Neuroscience	To let AI generate _____. Study neuroscience and cognitive science, trying to bridge _____ and _____.
Robot Learning: Perception and Manipulation	Build visual observation model, _____, and _____. Establish the mapping relationship between the _____ and the _____ by _____. Use knowledge base to _____, and then make robot _____.
Communion Service Robot, Evolutionary Computation	Do some restarch related to _____ & _____.
Visual AI, Autonomous Driving & Mobile Robotics	Focus on visual deep learning based methods for _____, autonomous navigation, and decision-making.
Information Retrieval & Recommendation	_____ a series of approaches on Advanced Web Search and Explainable Recommendation based on user modeling and users' satisfaction.
Machine Learning & AI Theory	Work on machine learning including probabilistic learning, adversarial robust machine learning, and also _____ _____.

2. Watch the video again, and take down the expressions used to describe research interest. One example has been given to you.

e.g., *I'm working on...*

_____

_____

_____

3. The video clip introduces Tsinghua's Artificial Intelligence Institute by the eight research teams and their directions. This is one way of introducing a research body. Discuss other ways of description with your partner.

Project

Suppose you are invited to introduce to a group of visiting scholars from Singapore your research and/or the research your team/school/institute focused on. Prepare a presentation of the introduction. If you can find a partner from the same team/school/institute, you can work together and make a joint presentation.

Unit 3

Making Presentations

Part I
Introducing the Unit

An academic presentation is an effective task that develops a student's communication skills. Students need to use these skills in their professional and personal lives in the future after studies. Therefore, academic presentations are becoming an important part of language learning, especially in the university environment. Presenting an academic topic in an engaging way is a win-win situation. Not only will your audience be less likely to fall asleep or become bored, but as a presenter, you can also be relieved of anxiety facing a crowd.

In this unit, we are going to present the basics about designing and making academic presentations, which will enable you to perform well in academic settings. You will listen to some presentations, analyze them, and then practice creating your own version.

Part II
Learning about the Activity

Making a good academic presentation is to give the audience a sense of what your work is, get feedback on your work and make the audience want to learn more about your research. It starts with crafting the content with an easy-to-follow structure. Besides, delivery is as important as the content. In order to ensure a smooth delivery, some factors (e.g., articulation, modulation, stage presence and non-verbal language) should be taken under the speaker's control.

→ Structure

An academic presentation can be broken down into three sections: an introduction, a body and a conclusion.

❶ Introduction

The introduction must grasp the audience's attention, identify the topic and provide a brief overview or agenda of what you will cover in the talk. Therefore, you need to explain why your work is interesting, place the study in context, use some pretty visuals or amazing facts to draw the audience's attention to the issue and questions you are addressing, and clearly state your topic.

❷ Body

The body is the part of the presentation between your introduction and your conclusion. It is the longest part of the presentation, and its purpose is to get your key points across. You need to talk about the sources and the research method, indicate if there are conflicting views about the subject, and make a statement about your new results. Also, you need to use visual aids or handouts if appropriate.

❸ Conclusion

The conclusion to your academic presentation is a great opportunity to reinforce the key message of your talk. You need to summarize the main points covered, conclude your talk, thank the audience for their attention and invite questions.

→ Delivery

Delivery is what you are probably most concerned about when it comes to giving presentations. A good speaker needs to be articulate and use words that are understandable. A good speaker also uses the right facial expressions and appropriate gestures. Moreover, speakers are expected to talk directly to the audience, maintaining eye contact with them. There are several principles to be followed.

❶ Articulation

When your words cannot be understood because of poor articulation, the presentation might as well not have been delivered at all. It is highly important to know the correct way of saying a word, no matter whether it is familiar or unfamiliar. Pronouncing the words correctly and clearly can ensure the effective transmission of your message.

❷ Modulation

Voice characteristics play a vital role in determining how the presentation is perceived. People like to listen to voices that are well-modulated, meaning the capability to adjust or manipulate the resonance and timbre of the vocal tone. Varying the speed at which you talk, and emphasizing changes in pitch and tone both help to make your voice more interesting and hold your audience's attention. As a presenter, you need a volume loud enough for the audience to hear the speech easily, but that does not mean you should use one loud volume only. Varying the volume holds the audience's attention. Changing the pitch also helps create interest. Besides, the delivery rate should be properly paced so that it is neither too fast to understand nor too slow to distract the audience.

❸ Stage presence

Stage presence is the ability of the speaker to fill the space and project his/her personality to the audience. The opposite of stage presence is stage fright; that is, you feel particularly nervous and anxious when you deliver a presentation. No one is immune from stage fright. Some people just manage it better than others and create what we see as stage presence. In order to overcome your stage fright, you need to think of yourself as someone who is sharing valuable information with willing listeners. In fact, a little nervousness can be a good thing that helps you to focus better.

❹ Using nonverbal language

It is not just the choice of words and their proper pronunciation that make an effective presentation delivery. The message of any presentation is reinforced, clarified, and complemented by nonverbal communication such as facial expressions, gestures, and movement. Without these nonverbal elements, you may be judged as boring, with flat delivery and an unemotional voice. Facial expressions should change with the content of the presentation. Gestures should emphasize only certain points. Movement should allow you to carry the presentation around, forward, and to the audience. It should also direct the audience to follow the speaker and keep them hanging on to his/her every word.

Part III
Learning Useful Expressions

→ Introduction

Greeting the audience

- Good morning/afternoon, ladies and gentlemen.

- Good morning/afternoon, everyone.

Expressing the topic/purpose

- My purpose/objective/aim today is...

- What I want to do this morning/afternoon/today is...

- I'm here today to...

Giving the structure

- This talk is divided into...main parts.

- To start with / Firstly, I'd like to look at...

- Then/Secondly, I'll be talking about...

- Thirdly...

- My fourth point will be about...

- Finally, I'll be looking at...

Giving the timing

- My presentation/talk will take/last about...minutes.

Handling questions

- At the end of my talk, there will be a chance to ask questions.

- I'll be happy to answer any questions you have at the end of my presentation.

→ Body

Visual aids

- As you can see here...

- Here we can see...

- If we look at this slide...

- This slide shows...

- If you look at the screen, you'll see...

- This table/diagram/chart/slide shows...

- I'd like you to look at this...

- Let's (have a) look at...

- On the right/left you can see...

Transitions

- Let's now move on to / turn to...

- I now want to go on to...

- This leads/brings me to my next point, which is...

- I'd now like to move on to / turn to...

- So far we have looked at...Now I'd like to...

Giving examples

- Let me give you an example...

- Such as...

- For instance...

- A good example of this is...

Summarizing

- What I'm trying to say is...

- Let me just try and sum that up before we move on to...

- So far, I've presented...

→ Conclusion

Summing up

- To summarize...

- So, to sum up...

- To recap...

- Let me now sum up.

Concluding

- Let me end by saying...

- I'd like to finish by emphasizing...

- In conclusion, I'd like to say...

- Finally, may I say...

Thanking the audience

- Thank you for your attention/time.

- Thank you (for listening / very much).

Inviting questions

- If you have any questions or comments, I'll be happy to answer them now.

- If there are any questions, I'll do my best to answer them.

- Are there any more questions?

Part IV
Practicing Listening

 Task 1

Watch the lecture "What Is a Good Academic Presentation?" by Aditi Jhaveri and complete the following exercises.

1. **Watch the lecture ONCE and fill in each blank with ONE word.**
   The speaker was discussing some key factors in an academic presentation.

   1) Key factor 1: _____

   2) Key factor 2: _____

   3) Key factor 3: _____

   4) Key factor 4: _____

   5) Key factor 5: _____

2. **Watch the lecture again and answer the following questions.**

1) How are references cited in an academic presentation?

_____

_____

2) What is signposting?

_____

_____

3) How can we make better slides?

_____

_____

4) How will you reduce nervousness when you deliver your presentation?

_____

_____

Task 2

Watch an excerpt from the lecture "Giving an Effective Poster Presentation" and complete the following exercises.

1. **Watch the video ONCE and fill in each blank with ONE word.**

What Are the Poster Sessions Like?

Poster sessions (1) _____ in very social and (2) _____ settings. There are often (3) _____ or hundreds of posters in very large rooms that have very little sound (4) _____ material. Plus, there are lots of people (5) _____ around often with food and drink. They are all talking to one another. So poster sessions can get really (6) _____ and really (7) _____. And they are absolutely going to be (8) _____ for you, especially for the first time.

2. **Watch again and answer the following questions.**

1) How many rules does the speaker suggest for an effective poster presentation? What are they?

_____

_____

_____

2) Is the speaker satisfied with the poster presenter's final performance? What are his comments?

_____

_____

_____

 Task 3

Watch the introduction of an academic presentation and complete the following exercises.

1. **Watch the video ONCE. Choose all the functions the speaker achieves in the introduction from the following list and put them in the correct order.**

   A. Greeting the audience.

   B. Presenting the outline.

   C. Giving the time.

   D. Introducing oneself and his/her partner.

   E. Revealing the topic.

   F. Explaining the significance of the topic.

   _____

2. **Watch the video again and fill in each blank with NO MORE THAN FIVE words.**

No.	Signpost expressions
1	My name is Polly Wang and this is my _____ Calip Chen.
2	As we know, oral presentation _____ of our study at university.
3	Clearly, knowing how to give good effective oral presentation is _____ for all of us.
4	This is _____ of our presentation this morning.
5	I'd like to divide the presentation which will _____ into three main parts.
6	_____, I'm going to look at how to plan your presentation. Then I'll _____ the ways in which you can organize and write up your ideas and information. _____, Calip will you some suggestions about how to communicate your message and conclude the presentation. _____, there will be a short Q&A session.

3.   Watch the video again. Then match each signpost expression in Exercise 2 with the corresponding function listed in Exercise 1 and fill in the following table.

Signpost expressions	Functions
1	
2	
3	
4	
5	
6	

Part V
Practicing Speaking

Task 1

Work in pairs. Watch a student's presentation in class and make some comments or suggestions on his performance.

Task 2

Work in pairs. Watch another presentation delivered by the same student the next week. Then discuss with your partner how he improved his performance.

Task 3

Work in pairs. Listen to the professor's feedback and discuss with your partner whether you agree with the professor.

Task 4

What is the most difficult thing about giving a presentation and how should we tackle the problem? Form a group with another pair of students and discuss the question.

Part VI
Performing the Activity

Situation 1

Work in groups. Watch a research presentation given by Emily Johnston and take notes. Take turns to retell the presentation to your group members in one minute based on the template below. Then discuss how the speaker presented her research ideas effectively in a short period of time.

In this presentation, the speaker mainly talked about...

First and foremost, she mentioned that...

She then discussed...

Moreover, she talked about...

She illustrated it by...

Last but not least, the speaker highlighted...

Situation 2

Suppose you and your partner take part in a poster session of an academic conference. You two present your poster to the viewers for two minutes. After your presentation, you answer their questions about the poster. You should present the posters and answer questions by following the steps below.

Step 1: Divide the whole class into groups of four. Each group is further divided into two subgroups.

Step 2: Each subgroup chooses a poster for their presentation.

Step 3: The two subgroups take turns to present their posters for two minutes. After each presentation, there is a Q&A session during which the presenters answer questions from their audience.

Exercises

Task 1

Watch a poster presentation given by the students from University of Rochester and complete the exercises.

1. Identify the structure of the poster presentation and complete the following table. One answer has been given as an example.

   Structure of a Poster Presentation

1	Title
2	
3	
4	
5	

2. How do the two presenters distribute their responsibilities in the presentation?

   _____

   _____

   _____

3. Work in pairs. Find and read more research poster samples from the Internet, and analyze their structures. Discuss with your partner what other parts might be included in a poster presentation.

Task 2

Work in groups. Watch a poster presentation given by a student named Jake Drysdale. Share your comments on it with your group members by answering the following questions.

1. **Overall visual: Are the components of the poster balanced across the space?**

    _____

    _____

    _____

2. **Overall organization: Are the components of the poster organized in a logical flow?**

    _____

    _____

    _____

3. **Overall delivery:**

    1) Does the presenter sufficiently explain the poster?

    _____

    2) Does the presenter speak clearly and distinctly?

    _____

    3) Does the presenter show enthusiasm about his topic?

    _____

Task 3

Watch a research presentation entitled "Suspects, Science and CSI" by Matthew Thompson and complete the following exercises.

1. **Watch the video ONCE and choose all the segments included in the presentation from the list below.**
    A. Introduction
    B. Thesis
    C. Literature Review
    D. Methods
    E. Results
    F. Future Directions

G. Limitations

H. Acknowledgement

_____

2.   **How did the speaker introduce the topic of his PhD thesis?**

_____

_____

_____

3.   **Watch the video again and fill in each blank with ONE word.**

My PhD thesis is about (1) _____ how examiners make these important (2) _____. In Australia alone, there are over 5,000 of these (3) _____ made per day to be used as (4) _____ in (5) _____ criminals. But (6) _____ mistakes are made. In 2004, a lawyer named Brandon Mayfield was (7) _____ by the FBI because his fingerprints (8) _____ those found on a bomb that (9) _____ killing (10) _____ people. But here's the catch. The fingerprint examiners made a mistake. They matched the print to the wrong person. Mayfield was (11) _____.

Task 4

Watch a research presentation given by Frob Duguid and complete the following exercises.

1.   **What is the starter of the presentation? Do you think the starter can hook the audience?**

_____

_____

_____

2. **Watch the video again. Then take down notes about the research methods, results and conclusion. Fill in the blanks with the information you hear.**

	Hypothesis		
Research methods / Experimental design	Independent variable (Cause)		
	Dependent variable (Effect)		
	Participants		
	Sample size		
	Experiment conditions	Experimental group	
		Control group	
Results			
Conclusion			

3. **Watch the presentation again and check your answers.**

 Task 5

The conclusion of your research presentation is a great opportunity to reinforce the key message or the finding of your talk. Watch a mini-lecture entitled "How to End a Presentation?" and answer the following questions.

1. **What alternative ways can you use to close the presentation rather than "That's all. Thank you"?**

_____

_____

_____

2. **How do non-verbal skills affect the ending of your presentation?**

_____

_____

_____

3. **The following is an example of the ending of a presentation. Rehearse it to your classmates by following the tips given in the lecture, and ask them for suggestions.**

"In summary, our society would be healthier if more people took part in sports of all kinds. We should continue to try to prevent accidents and injuries. However, we should also ensure that sports are challenging, exciting, and, above all, fun. Thank you. "

📖 Project

Work in groups. Each group is going to choose a research topic that they are interested in and give a presentation of a research proposal. Your presentation will be based on your own or someone else's research. The proposal should be presented in four to five slides within five minutes. It is suggested that the slides include the following information: (1) the title page; (2) some general background information about your topic; (3) research questions or hypothesis; (4) theoretical descriptions or methodology; and (5) expected outcomes. Each group presents their research ideas to the whole class and asks for feedback and suggestions.

Unit 4

Answering Questions

Part I
Introducing the Unit

Answering the audience's questions after presentation is an excellent way to clarify and reinforce your research ideas. Therefore, the question and answer (Q&A) period is actually another presentation and vital to most speaking situations. However, as impromptu speaking is the worst fear of many, dealing with questions from audience can be one of the most difficult aspects of presenting your research.

In this unit, we are going to learn a few strategies to cope with audience questions so that you will be able to stay confidently in control. You will analyze some examples of responding to questions, and then practice handling questions on your own.

Part II
Learning about the Activity

In addition to the pressure of speaking in front of a crowd of academic peers, questions are often difficult to answer for a number of reasons: communication difficulties, lack of information, inability to understand the exact question, or even difficulty to hear the questioner clearly. But that does not mean you cannot prepare for the Q&A session in advance and make it a productive part of your presentation. Answering questions provides another opportunity for you to ensure shared meaning and meet your listeners' needs. The following guidelines provide a comprehensive approach to answering questions you are likely to encounter during your research presentations and give you some advice on how to respond to these difficult questions and awkward situations.

→ Structure

There are three things you need to do when you answer questions. You need to check questions, respond to questions and conclude questions.

❶ Check questions

First, you should listen to the entire questions and make sure you understand what is being asked. You may need to rephrase the question and ask, "Did I understand you correctly?" You can repeat the question only if necessary. If someone asks a question in a large audience without using a microphone or if your presentation is being taped, you will need to repeat the question.

❷ Respond to questions

When you start responding to a question, you need to talk to the audience, not just the questioner. You should begin by addressing the questioner, then turn to others in the audience. When you finish, give eye contact to other audience and ask, "Who else has a question?" You need to answer the question as directly and briefly as possible without being abrupt. You can use your answers to reinforce your main points. If you do not know the answer, do not be afraid to say, "I don't know, but I'll get back to you with the answer." You can postpone questions that require lengthy answers. Give a brief answer or admit that there is more to be said, and offer to discuss it more fully in private. You need to take control of the situation, deciding when to move on.

❸ Conclude questions

After you have answered the last question, you need to wrap up your presentation with a one-or-two-sentence summary. You'd better not simply say "thank you" and leave.

→ Principles

Once you receive a question, you will have a few moments to think about it and reframe it in a way that makes sense to you. There are five principles on how to react—you can answer, reflect, deflect, defer or change the scope of the question. Once you have answered concisely, you can then follow up to check if the questioner is satisfied and then continue.

❶ Answer

If you have a good answer to the question from the audience, go ahead and keep it short and clear.

❷ Reflect

You can ask a question back to the audience member, such as "Can you clarify what you mean by that?". You can also dismiss the question if it is irrelevant to the issue, factually inaccurate, personal or based on false assumptions. But you should be careful when using this method.

❸ Deflect

You can ask the question back to the audience or pass it to another panel member if possible. Another technique is to imply that the question has been asked already, which means you do not want to cover old ground.

❹ Defer

You can tell the audience that you will talk to them after the event. This gives you more time to think of a good answer and less pressure to give a perfect answer. You can also mention that the answer is coming up in a slide.

❺ Adjust

This involves answering the question but changing the subject. You can also give a partial answer or give a negative answer, saying that something else will happen instead. You can avoid answering questions that are beyond the scope of your talk by saying: "I'm afraid that it really falls outside of my objectives for today's presentation. Perhaps we can resume discussion of that particular point later."

Part III
Learning Useful Expressions

→ Fielding questions

When you don't hear the question well

*   Sorry, I couldn't hear that. Could you say it louder please?

*   Sorry, I couldn't hear that very well. Could you repeat it a bit louder?

*   Sorry, I didn't hear the last part of your question. Could you repeat that part again please?

*   Sorry, I couldn't hear all of your questions. Did you say/ask "..."?

*   Pardon? I couldn't quite hear the last part of the sentence. Are you asking

whether/if...?

When you don't understand the question fully (or you aren't asked a clear question)

- Sorry, I didn't understand the question. Could you repeat it please?

- Sorry, I didn't quite catch your question/meaning there.

- Sorry, I couldn't understand the last part (of your question).

- Sorry, I'm not sure (that) I understand. Did you say/ask/mean "..."?

- Sorry, I'm not quite sure of your question. Are you asking if/whether...?

When you need a little thinking time before giving your answer

- Good question...Well...(start your answer)

- Good point...Well...

- That's a good/interesting question...OK...

- Ah, yes...OK...that's a good point...

- Ah, that's interesting...Let me think (a second)...

- Let me consider the best way to answer that.

- That point deserves some thought. Let's see...

→ Responding to questions

When you want to emphasize you are giving a tentative answer only

- My first thoughts are that...

- Off the top of my head (maybe)...

- I'm not sure what the research says on this, but maybe...

- That's a bit beyond the scope of this talk, but my understanding is that basically...

- I'm summarizing here, so some details may differ, but...

When you do not know the answer and do not want to give a tentative one

- I don't have the data here / at hand (right now), and I need to check it before answering.

- I'm not sure what the answer to that is, and I don't want to mislead anyone, so I don't think I can answer that right now.

- I know that A and B are researching that, but I don't know what they've found.

- That's beyond the scope of this research, and I'm not sure how to give a reasonable answer. But that's an interesting point.

- That would be interesting to find out, but I don't know the answer. Thank you for raising the question.

- That might be more in the field of X, and I'm not that familiar with it enough to answer.

- Can I email it to you later? / I'll email you (in the next few days / later today /... if you give me your email address).

- (If you email me at this address,) I'll answer your question as quickly as I can.

When you disagree with the asker

- It seems we think differently. Maybe we can talk more later.

- I understand your point, but I believe my approach offers a new way forward as I explained...

- I think this comes down to a difference in theoretical basis, which we're not going to be able to resolve during this Q&A. Maybe we can talk more later about this.

- I'm not sure that's correct, but I'll look it up and we can discuss it later.

- Thanks for the comment/question. It's something for me to think about.

Part IV
Practicing Listening

Task 1

Watch a mini-lecture "How to Handle Difficult Questions?" by Matt Abrahams and complete the following exercises.

1. **Watch the video ONCE. Then take down some notes about the different types of difficult questions and fill in each blank with NO MORE THAN THREE words.**

Four Types of Difficult Questions

Situation 1	The audience ask a question and you don't _____ .
Situation 2	_____ questioning (The questioner asks several questions one after the other.)
Situation 3	Individuals don't ask a question. They make a _____ because they don't know how to ask a question or they want to show they know a lot about what you are speaking on and try to _____ from you.
Situation 4	You get a question _____ .

2. **In the video, some tips are given for each question type. Watch the video again and match the tips with the different question types.**

Situation 1 (   ) A. You can pick one or two that you remember and answer them. Or you can ask the question asker to repeat the question.

Situation 2 (   ) B. You simply say, "I don't know."

Situation 3 (   ) C. You can say, "It seems that you have a lot of passion on this topic", or "I hear there is a great concern in your voice", and go ahead to paraphrase the question.

Situation 4 (   ) D. Instead of looking at the person, you can turn yourself to take question from another part of the audience.

3. Watch the video again and list the benefits of dealing with difficult questions effectively.

_____

_____

_____

Task 2

At a thesis defense, the defense committee members ask the student questions after the student gives a presentation of his or her findings. It is highly challenging for the student to respond effectively to the defense committee during the Q&A period. Watch an excerpt from the lecture "The Perfect Defense: The Oral Defense of a Dissertation" by Dr. Valerie Balester and answer the following questions.

1. **What difficult situations did Dr. Valerie Balester address in her lecture?**

_____

_____

_____

2. **What solutions did she offer the student to deal with each difficult situation?**

_____

_____

_____

3. **What happens after the committee members have asked all their questions?**

_____

_____

_____

Task 3

Watch a mini-lecture "10 Mistakes to Avoid when Defending Your Thesis" and complete the following exercises.

1. **Watch the video ONCE. Then choose the mistakes that are not mentioned by the speaker from the following list.**
    A. Avoiding eye contact when questioned.

B. Being arrogant.

C. Attending mock thesis defenses.

D. Pretending to know the answer when you don't.

E. Rushing yourself before the defense.

F. Challenging the questioner.

---

2. **Watch the video again. Then note down some details from the lecture and fill in each blank with NO MORE THAN THREE words.**

Situations	Useful expressions
Asking for clarifications when the question is unclear.	My apologies but I'm afraid I didn't catch the _____ of your question. Can you please help me better understand _____ when you said this or that?
Avoiding rambling on and on.	Thank you for the question. It's a very good question. In _____, there are three _____ that _____. Firstly, ...Secondly, ...Thirdly, ...Does that _____ your question? Thank you.

3. **Watch the video again and decide whether the following statements are true (T) or false (F).**

   1) You can let the questioners finish their questions because they might feel they are important when they talk. ( )

   2) You can suppress your nervousness by disagreeing with whatever the questioner says. ( )

   3) At the oral defense, speaking too slowly is worse than speaking too fast. ( )

   4) You can attend some thesis defenses prior to your own in order to get familiar with the whole process. ( )

   5) You can be spontaneous in speaking after you read your own thesis thoroughly. ( )

Part V
Practicing Speaking

Task 1

Work in pairs. Watch a video of an oral defense and make some comments or suggestions on the student's performance.

Task 2

Work in pairs. Watch a video of another oral defense given by the same student. Then discuss with your partner how the student improved her performance in the defense.

Task 3

Form a group with another pair of students and discuss some rules students should follow in order to do properly in the Q&A period of a thesis defense.

Task 4

Share your group's ideas with the rest of the class.

Part VI
Performing the Activity

Situation 1

Suppose you have finished your presentation, and are moving on to the Q&A stage. Unfortunately nobody asks a question even though you invite questions. Discuss in groups and work out some ways to deal with the awkward situation. Each group decides on the best way to encourage questions from the audience and share it with the whole class.

Step 1: Form a group of four students.

Step 2: Each group member will take turns to present his/her ideas.

Step 3: As a group, discuss and select the best way to deal with the awkward situation.

Step 4: Each group will report the group's decision to the class.

Situation 2

Suppose you participate in a symposium. As a presenter, you should answer questions from the audience after you finish your presentation. As a member of the audience, you are expected to ask questions after you listen to the other speakers' presentations. Divide the whole class into two groups. The two groups take turns to ask and answer questions by following the four steps below.

Step 1: Read the abstract of Research A.

Group 1 will anticipate questions from Group 2.

Group 2 will prepare questions to ask Group 1.

Step 2: Conduct Q&A session for Research A.

Step 3: Read the abstract of Research B.

Group 1 will prepare questions to ask Group 2.

Group 2 will anticipate questions from Group 1.

Step 4: Conduct Q&A session for Research B.

Research A

Title: Life-and-Death Attitude and Its Formation Process and End-of-Life Care Expectations Among the Elderly Under Traditional Chinese Culture: A Qualitative Study

Abstract

Introduction

With the global aging process intensified, the demand for end-of-life care has surged, especially in China. However, its development is restricted. Understanding the life and death attitude among the elderly and its formation process, and clarifying their needs, are so important to promote social popularization of end-of-life care.

Methodology

This qualitative study included 20 elderly residents in Nan and Shuangbei

Communities, Chongqing City, People's Republic of China. Data were collected through semistructured in-depth individual interviews and processed by thematic analysis method.

Results

Three themes and eight subthemes were identified: characteristics of formation process (passive thinking, closed and single), life-and-death attitude (cherish and enjoy life, quality of life priority, let death take its course) and expectations of end-of-life care (preferences, basic needs, good death).

Discussion

Life-and-death attitude and end-of-life care expectations of the elderly support the development and delivery of end-of-life care. Furthermore, the individual-family-hospital linkage discussion channel needs to be further explored.

(Lei, L., Gan, Q. X., Gu, C. Y., Tan, J., & Luo, Y. 2021. Life-and-death attitude and its formation process and end-of-life care expectations among the elderly under traditional Chinese culture: a qualitative study. *Journal of Transcultural Nursing*, 6(1): 1-8.)

Research B

Title: As the Two-Child Policy Beckons: Work–Family Conflicts, Gender Strategies and Self-Worth Among Women from the First One-Child Generation in Contemporary China

Abstract

How do women from the one-child generation make fertility choices and negotiate work–family relationships under the two-child policy? I address this question by using 82 in-depth interviews with siblingless women from the first one-child cohort. This study unifies Gerson and Peiss's and Kandiyoti's conceptual frameworks on boundaries and gender strategies but adds a new dimension of self-worth. The data reveal three different fertility strategies: rejection, acceptance and procrastination, each representing different negotiations with patriarchal boundaries and assessment of self-worth. In particular, the findings highlight how the patriarchal tactics—within the state, the workplace and individual family— are coordinated and transformed into widely available discourse on fertility duties, meritocracy and productivity, thus maintaining rigid patriarchal boundaries across private and public spheres. Rather than being subservient to multifaceted patriarchal power, women strategies to evaluate and validate their competing work– family identities through the language of moral, financial and/or status worthiness.

(Liu, Y. 2021. As the two-child policy beckons: work–family conflicts, gender strategies and self-worth among women from the first one-child generation in contemporary China. *Work, Employment and Society*, *1*: 1–19.)

Task 1

Watch an excerpt from the Q&A with Elon Musk and complete the following exercises.

1. **Listen to the first questioner's questions and Elon Musk's responses. Fill in each blank with ONE word.**

    Question: If normal people want to travel to Mars, do we need some (1) _____ _____, or can normal people go there?

    Response: No, I mean we're trying to make it such that anyone can go.

    Question: Yeah, I know. But do we need, like, a lot of (2) _____ or something (3) _____?

    Response: (4) _____. Maybe a few days of training.

2. **Listen to the second questioner's questions and Elon Musk's responses. Answer the following questions.**

    1) What do the audience's questions focus on?

    _____

    _____

    _____

    2) What is the point of establishing a base on Mars?

    _____

    _____

    _____

    3) Why did Elon Musk make an analogy between doing interstellar travel and developing spacecraft?

    _____

    _____

    _____

3. **Work in pairs. Compare Elon Musk's responses to the two askers' questions. Discuss with your partner why Elon Musk gave short answers to the first asker's questions but long answers to the second asker's questions.**

Task 2

Watch a video of students giving a presentation and do the exercises below.

1. **Create a list of possible questions that the presenter might be asked at the Q&A session.**

2. **Work with your partner. Take turns to ask and answer each other's questions.**

Task 3

Watch the Q&A session of a presentation. Notice what the students say and do during the Q&A and complete the following exercises.

1. **Take down some notes about the questions as well as the answers, and fill in each blank with NO MORE THAN FOUR words.**

Questions	Answers
As you said at the beginning of the presentation, the growth of the elderly population in China will be more significant in the future. Could you tell us why it is more significant as developed countries have _____ as well?	What makes the growth of the elderly population in China significant is the _____ of the growth. In most of the European countries, like France, they have taken centuries to _____ the elderly population. But China only needed _____ years to do the same.
As far as I see, many Chinese people believe in _____. They _____ _____ their parents at home by themselves. So can you tell us why there will be a surge in _____ for elderly services in the future?	In the past century, elderly care services were mainly provided by _____, which means Chinese people were taking care of their own parents. This was possible because most of the _____ had more than one child. But the family structure has changed after all these years. The new family structure will be 4-2-1 structure, which means there are four _____, two parents, and one child. The only child in the family wouldn't be able to take care of his/her grandparents and his/her parents at the same time.

2. Note down the expressions used by the presenters to perform the following functions and complete the table below.

Functions	Expressions
Inviting questions.	
Thanking the questioner.	
Checking if the questioner is satisfied.	
Inviting more questions.	
Praising the questioner.	

3. Do you think the students' body language helps them to communicate effectively? If yes, how?

_____

_____

_____

Task 4

Watch two Q&A videos and complete the following exercises.

1. Note down the two questions and fill in the blanks of the table below.

Question 1	
Question 2	

2. Which question do you think is more difficult for the presenters to answer? And why?

_____

_____

_____

3. Watch the videos again and pay attention to the different ways of handling questions. Choose the steps taken by the two groups to answer questions from the following list.

A. Thanking the questioner.

B. Acknowledging the question.

C. Answering the question.

D. Deflecting.

E. Acknowledging the importance of the audience's questions.

F. Checking if the audience is satisfied.

The first group: _____

The second group: _____

 ## Task 5

Watch a video of poster networking sessions at FEMS2019 and complete the following exercises.

1. **Write down all the four questions the poster presenters answered.**

   Question 1: _____

   Question 2: _____

   Question 3: _____

   Question 4: _____

2. **Watch again. Then take down some notes about the poster presenters' answers to the second question and fill in each blank with ONE word.**

   Three Words to Summarize Their Experience in FEMS 2019

Presenter 1	_____; lots of _____ opportunities; _____
Presenter 2	_____; a _____ opportunity to get behind the scenes and _____ the conference
Presenter 3	_____; _____; _____

3. **Work in groups. Write down more general questions the poster presenters might be asked. Share your questions with your group members. Each group should list at least 5 of the most commonly asked questions.**

📝 Project

Work in groups and choose a research topic of interest to you all. Find a journal article on the topic online. Read it through in advance and prepare a group presentation sharing the research study you have read. As a group, you give a 10-minute presentation to the whole class first and then answer questions from your classmates after your presentation. Each group uses the following rubric to rate other groups' responses to questions in every category on a scale of 1 to 3.

Rubric for Answering Questions

	1	2	3
Subject Knowledge	The student shows a lack of knowledge by answering questions with little details or elaboration.	The student shows adequate knowledge by answering questions with certain details or elaboration.	The student demonstrates full knowledge by answering questions with sufficient explanations or elaboration.
Delivery: Fielding Questions	The student is uninterested and listens inattentively.	The student listens carefully but rarely restates the question.	The student listens carefully to the question and repeats it to confirm that he/she heard it correctly.
Delivery: Responding to Questions	The student has poor enunciation and the response is inaudible. The student gives very short responses.	The student answers the questions with good enunciation and pace. But he/she is occasionally able to adjust the answers to different questions.	The student speaks clearly and loudly. The student keeps the answer succinct. When a longer answer is required, the student suggests meeting the questioner after the symposium.
Physicality	The student's body movement is too much or too little. The student displays little eye contact or facial expressions.	The student's body movement is appropriate to the context. The student makes regular eye contact with audience and varies facial expressions.	The student customizes body movement and gestures to the context and topic. The student engages audience with varied and compelling eye contact and facial expressions.
Evidence/ Research	The student is not able to use appropriate evidence or experiences to support the answers.	The student is occasionally able to use evidence and experiences to answer questions.	The student is able to use specific evidence and experiences to answer questions.

Scoring Sheet for Answering Questions

Group	Subject Knowledge	Delivery: Fielding Questions	Delivery: Responding to Questions	Physicality	Evidence/ Research	Total Score
1						
2						
3						
4						
...						

Unit 5

Joining a Discussion

Part I
Introducing the Unit

As an important method to encourage participants to exchange information as well as thoughts and ideas, and thus to sparkle more creative ideas, discussions have become an essential, or even an integral part of academic activities such as seminars. To make a discussion successfully, you should be aware of what and how to speak in it.

In this unit, we are going to present the basic rules and skills about joining a discussion as well as some expressions you can use in a discussion. You will learn some examples of group discussions and then practice on your own.

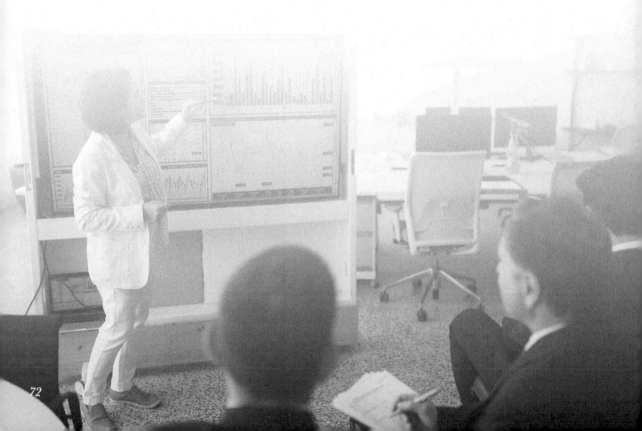

Part II
Learning about the Activity

→ What

Discussions can be carried out in pairs or in groups. Whatever the form, participants in discussions are advised to:

- be polite during the discussion, especially when having different opinions with each other;
- be active in the discussion instead of remaining silence;
- express their opinions in turn instead of being dominant;
- focus on the topic instead of chatting on something irrelevant.

Usually there will be a time limit for a discussion and so the participants, or at least one of them, should keep track of time. When discussing in groups, each member is advised to take a role, such as the facilitator or the leader, the timekeeper, the recorder, or the presenter, to make the discussion more productive.

→ How

The following are some tips on effective discussion skills.

Before the discussion

- Get familiar with the topic and have good subject knowledge. If you are not familiar with the topic, you may not be able to understand what the other participants are saying, and thus you may not make appropriate responses. In addition, you would be unable to express your ideas if you don't know about the topic.
- Arrive early. This may give you some time to talk with the other participants, which may help you to know their speaking manner, or even what they might say in the discussion. This may help you to have a better understanding of their speaking.
- Learn and prepare some expressions that can be used in the discussion, such as those to show agreement or disagreement.

During the discussion

- Take the initiative in speaking, especially when you are not so confident in expressing your opinion. You may start the discussion by introducing the topic and asking for other participants' opinions, which may help you to formulate your opinion.

- Listen actively to what other participants are saying. This can help you to identify the main ideas being discussed, to evaluate what is being said, and thus to help you stay attentive and focused.

- Take notes when necessary. During listening to other participants, note down their main points, and this may help you to respond to their opinions more successfully.

- Use appropriate expressions to voice your opinion, showing agreement or disagreement. Try not to interrupt the other speaker. If you do need to interrupt, use body language such as raising your hand to indicate that you want to interrupt first, and then use expressions such as "Sorry to interrupt, but I want to..." to make it more polite.

- Be cooperative during the discussion. Express your opinions in turn instead of remaining silent or keeping talking all the time.

Learn and practice the strategies and skills mentioned above, and you are sure to gain your confidence in making a successful discussion.

Part III
Learning Useful Expressions

→ Starting a discussion

- Today we are going to talk about...

- Let's start with...

- Who wants to be the first?

- Let me express my opinion first.

➔ Keeping the discussion going

* ... (the previous speaker) mentioned that...Do you agree, ...(the next speaker)?

* What do you think about what...has just mentioned?

* Who will be the next to give opinions?

➔ Making a summary

* Okay, so we've talked about...

* As mentioned by (the previous speaker), ...

* In conclusion, ...

* To sum up, we have looked at...

* Before we close, let me just summarize the main points being mentioned.

* Well, that's enough to think about today.

➔ Voicing an opinion

* From what I understand, ...

* I think/believe that...

* As far as I am concerned, ...

➔ Giving evidence

* For example/instance, ...

* This can be seen by...

* Statistics from...indicate that...

➔ Showing agreement

* Well, I agree with...

* That's true. / Yeah, so true.

- Yeah, I also think that...

- I think that's a great idea.

- I take your point.

- That's how I see it.

→ Showing disagreement

- Sorry, but I don't think...

- I have a different opinion on what...has just said.

- I'm afraid I can't agree with...

- That's not always the case, because...

→ Adding a different opinion

- I agree to some extent, but...

- I agree with..., but I want to talk about another major cause of...

- Besides what...has just mentioned, I think..., too.

→ Interrupting

- Sorry for interrupting, but can I just say/mention/add something here?

- Before you move on, I'd like to say something.

→ Responding to the interruption

- Is there something you would like to say?

- Let me finish what I was saying, please.

- I am almost finished my point.

Part IV
Practicing Listening

Task 1

Watch the video "How to Get Better in Group Discussions" and complete the following exercises.

1. **Note down the six tips that are mentioned in the video.**

   1) _____

   2) _____

   3) _____

   4) _____

   5) _____

   6) _____

2. **Watch the video again for details and complete the following table with the information you get.**

Tips	What you are advised to do	Why you are advised to do so
1	Review _____ Make _____ Read _____ Become aware of _____ _____	(Not being mentioned in the video.)
2	Show up _____	Give _____ _____ Meet _____ _____ Feel _____ _____
3	Not to use _____ Not to use _____	Qualifiers: _____ _____ Tag questions: _____ _____

(Continued)

Tips	What you are advised to do	Why you are advised to do so
4	Your voice should sound _____ _____	A soft tone: • conveys _____ • may not allow _____ _____
5	Acknowledge _____ _____ Provide _____ _____	Make your idea _____ _____
6	Express _____ Share _____ _____	You may still have something to say.

Task 2

Watch the video "Successful Group Discussion Techniques" and learn some expressions that can be used in a group discussion.

1. **Watch the first part of the video and fill in each blank with the information you hear from the video.**

    Group discussion is not a (1) _____. In group discussion, we neither (2) _____ the topic nor (3) _____. Moreover, there are no (4) _____ positions or (5) _____ to be taken. Group discussion is a (6) _____ discussion and a (7) _____ interaction in which you examine a subject or a problem from different (8) _____ and viewpoints.

2. **Watch the rest part of the video with focus on the expressions. Decide in which situations you can use the following expressions and complete the table.**

    a. It is quite clear to me that...

    b. This is just what I also think.

    c. Please allow me to defer.

    d. Could we stick to the subject please?

    e. What I think is...

    f. May I make a point about...

g. I am in complete agreement with...

h. I am convinced that...

When to Use the Above Expressions

Situations	Expressions
1)	
2) When supporting the views of other participants	b, g
3)	
4)	
5)	

3.   **Share in a group the other expressions you know that can be used in the five situations mentioned in this video.**

Task 3

To make the group discussion more effective, each member in the group is often suggested to take a role. Watch the video "The Roles of Members in a Group Discussion" and complete the following exercises.

1.   **Match the following roles of members in a group discussion with their specific tasks.**

Roles

Tasks

1) Facilitator   a. To share what the group came up with.

2) Timekeeper   b. To keep the group focused and participating in discussion.

3) Recorder   c. To summarize and write down the thoughts of the group.

4) Presenter   d. To remind the group of using the time well.

2.   **Decide whether the following statements are true (T) or false (F) according to the video.**

1) Usually there are four members in a group discussion.   (   )

2) Each member is advised to take a different role to make sure the discussion is productive.   (   )

3) The leader of the group only needs to organize the discussion and doesn't need to join in the discussion.   (   )

4) It's advised to spend some time thinking about the question and the opinions before the discussion.   (   )

3. Usually there is a time limit for a group discussion. Discuss in groups how the time can be used in a group discussion by following the example of a 7-minute discussion mentioned in the video.

Of the 10 minutes:

_____ minutes for _____

_____ minutes for _____

_____ minutes for _____

Part V
Practicing Speaking

Task 1

Work in groups and discuss your understanding of the different roles in a group discussion that are mentioned in the video "The Roles of Members in a Group Discussion". Then share within the group which role you usually take or you'd like to take during a group discussion.

Task 2

Work in groups of four and each member takes a role: Facilitator, Timekeeper, Recorder, or Presenter. Then make a 7-minute discussion on the topic "How to Make a Successful Group Discussion".

Task 3

Make a 3-minute presentation on the topic "How to Participate in a Group Discussion Successfully" with reference to the information you have learnt from the previous parts in this unit.

Part VI
Performing the Activity

Situation 1

Suppose you are going to attend a seminar. Work in groups and discuss what you can do to prepare for the discussion.

Step 1: Divide the whole class into groups with four members in each group.

Step 2: Nominate each member in each group for one of the following roles: Facilitator, Timekeeper, Recorder, or Presenter.

Step 3: Students carry out discussion in each group for five minutes.

Step 4: Ask one group or two to present the results of their discussion.

Situation 2

Work in groups and share your own experience of joining discussions. Were these discussions successful or unsuccessful and why? What kind of problems do you have when joining discussions? What can you do to improve your discussion skills?

Step 1: Divide the whole class into groups with four members in each group.

Step 2: Nominate each member in each group for one of the following roles: Facilitator, Timekeeper, Recorder, or Presenter.

Step 3: Students carry out discussion in each group for five minutes.

Step 4: Ask students which groups have experienced successful discussions and which groups have experienced unsuccessful discussions.

Step 5: Ask one group to share their experience of successful discussions or one group to share their experience of unsuccessful discussions.

Step 6: (If students present the experience of successful discussions) Ask the whole class why the discussion experience being mentioned is successful.
(If students present the experience of unsuccessful discussions) Ask the whole class why the discussion experience being mentioned is unsuccessful and what can be done to improve the discussion.

📖 Exercises

Task 1

Watch a video clip and learn how to interrupt politely in a conversation.

1. **List in NO MORE THAN FOUR words the situations that are mentioned in this video when people interrupt in a conversation.**

   1) When someone is _____

   2) When someone keeps _____

   3) When you want to _____

   4) When you want to _____

2. **Work in pairs and explain your understanding of the situations mentioned in the video.**

3. **It is suggested at the end of this video clip that we need to interrupt politely. Discuss in pairs how we interrupt politely.**

Task 2

As is suggested in Task 1, when we need to interrupt in a conversation, we do it politely. And it is also important for us to respond politely when we are interrupted. Watch another video by Emma to learn how to respond politely to interruption.

1. **Choose the best answer to each of the following questions according to what Emma said in the video.**

   1) What can you do when you are interrupted?

      A. You just keep talking and ignore the interruption.

      B. You need to stop your talking and give the turn to others.

      C. You can tell the other person politely that you want to finish your talking first.

      D. You can tell the other person that it's rude to interrupt one's talking.

   2) Which of the following expressions is NOT appropriate in responding to interruption?

      A. Let me finish what I was saying.

B. Is there something you would like to add?

C. I'm almost finished with my point.

D. Don't interrupt me, OK?

2. **It is mentioned in this video that sometimes we use body language to communicate. Watch the last part of the video and find out the examples of body language people use for interruption.**

Body language used when someone wants to interrupt:

_____

_____

_____

Body language used to stop someone's interruption:

_____

_____

_____

Task 3

Watch a video on successful and unsuccessful group discussions and complete the following exercises.

1. **Watch the first part of the video and discuss in groups why the group discussion is unsuccessful.**

2. **Watch the second part of the video and list out the changes to make the discussion successful.**

_____

_____

_____

3. **Discuss in groups what kind of problems you also have in your group discussion. Which suggestions would you adopt to improve your group discussion? Share with each other your opinions and give reasons.**

Task 4

Watch the video "How to Discuss a Topic in a Group" to learn some expressions that can be used to make a successful group discussion.

1. **List out the expressions used in the video for the following functions.**

• To start the discussion:	• To end the discussion:
• To clarify one's own opinion:	• To add something:
• To show agreement:	• To show disagreement:
•To interrupt:	• To hold the floor:

2. **Discuss in groups on the following questions.**

    1) Is there anything not so appropriate in the group discussion?

    2) How would you carry out your discussion if you were given the same topic? Would you have the same problems? Would you have other problems? What can you do to solve these problems?

Task 5

Watch one example of group discussion on insomnia to see how such discussion is carried out.

1. **Decide whether the following statements are true (T) or false (F) according to the video.**

    1) The first speaker was the leader of the discussion and she didn't join in the discussion. ( )

    2) The other members of the group expressed their opinions in turn. ( )

    3) The members only expressed their own opinions without responding to others' opinions. ( )

    4) The members disagreed with each other as they mentioned different causes of insomnia. ( )

2. **What do you think of this group discussion? Work in groups and share your opinions within your group.**

📖 Project

Work in groups. Suppose you are going to attend a seminar on online education. The issue is whether it is better to study online or in a regular classroom. First, find some related articles from the Internet as your references and formulate your own opinion. Then, hold a group discussion to see whether you agree with each other.

Unit **6**

Raising Questions

Part I
Introducing the Unit

Questions are sometimes more valuable than answers as asking questions enables people to organize their thinking around what they do not know, which may inspire innovations and breakthroughs. Asking questions in a class, a lecture, or a conference can be equal to a three-way discussion between the questioner, the speaker, and the audience. For this reason, raising questions is encouraged in academic settings such as classes, lectures, seminars as well as the Q&A sessions at conferences.

In this unit, we are going to present some basic principles on how to raise questions as well as the different types of questions that are often asked in academic settings. You will watch some video examples of raising questions in seminars or conferences, and then practice by following these examples.

Part II
Learning about the Activity

Though it is natural to hesitate to ask questions in public due to the shy personality, exhaustion after sitting and listening for a long time, or other reasons, it is strongly suggested that we ask questions when attending lectures, seminars or conferences as the questions may not only help deepen the comprehension of the questioner, and the other members of the audience, too, but also motivate the speaker to refine his/her lecture or presentation when answering questions.

To raise questions, especially good questions in academic settings, you need courage, and more importantly, strategies that can help you to raise questions appropriately. The following is a list of such tips.

❶ Get prepared before attending the lecture, the seminar, or the conference

A very good method to gain confidence is to make full preparation. Before attending a class, a lecture, a seminar, or a conference, you can preview what might be mentioned in the setting through the study of relevant materials, such as the course book, reference materials on the topic, or the publications of the speaker. During the preview, you can think about some questions in advance and if some of them remain unsolved at the end, you may choose one to raise in the Q&A session.

❷ Listen actively

During the listening, try to be an active listener. Do not simply absorb information, but keep thinking actively. For example, you can compare the information being mentioned with what you have in your brain, and try to make connections between them. Once you develop this habit, you may find that questions begin to come up automatically from your active thinking. Besides, note-taking is an essential part of active listening. You can not only take notes on the important information, but also the questions that come up during your thinking, and in this way your notes can be a good source of the questions to be raised.

❸ Ask specific questions

Sometimes you may see people at a conference making long-winded comments instead of asking a question. This is not productive, as the presenter and the audience may all look forward to questions, especially those good ones that may further elaborate the presentation, and the commentary would be saved for a written response or a private conversation afterwards. So, do try to ask an actual question instead of making long comments.

You can ask questions for the following purposes:

- to ask for repetition;

- to ask for clarification;

- to ask for more information;

- to present different opinions.

No matter what the purpose is, just remember that it is helpful to the presenter if you ask something specific. If a presentation contains multiple topics, it is particularly important to begin your questions by specifying the topic that your questions will be addressing.

In addition, it is necessary to keep your questions short and to the point as you need to save time for the other audience to raise questions.

❹ Be polite

Your questions should be presented in a professional and polite way by using appropriate expressions and speaking manners. Questions do not necessarily need to be critical, and you should not be combative though you are free to disagree with the speaker or to challenge his/her opinions. Show respect to the speaker and ask questions as you would like to have them asked to you.

❺ Keep practicing

Asking questions is an essential activity in academic career. Aim to ask at least one question at each academic setting you attend. The more questions you ask, the better you will be at asking questions.

Part III
Learning Useful Expressions

→ Remarks before raising a question

- Thank you so much for such a wonderful lecture! I am quite interested in the...you've just mentioned. Could you please...?

- Your speech has deeply impressed me, especially..., and I just wonder whether you could...

- I am fascinated by your description of your study, but I still have a question about...

→ Specifying the theme of the question

- Dear Chairman, I'd like to ask...a question.

- You mentioned...in your presentation, and I have a question about...

→ Following up other questions

- I'd like to follow up on the previous question.

- I am also interested in the question that is raised by...Could you please give more details on...?

→ Responding to answers

- Yes, I got it. Thank you!

- Thanks, that's clear now.

- That's not really what I was asking. What I meant was...

- Perhaps I didn't make my question clear. What I was really asking was...

→ Asking for clarification

- Perhaps I have missed something from your talk. Would you please explain...?

- I don't quite understand what you really mean by saying that...Can you please elaborate on it again?

- Could you please turn to your slide Page xx...? I noticed...on that slide. What does that mean?

- You have just mentioned that...Could you give me an example?

→ Asking for additional information

- Could you expand a bit on what you were saying about...?

- I am not familiar with this field, would you mind saying a few more words about...?

→ Raising different opinions or suggestions

- If I am not mistaken, you said that...However, the study published on the journal...has suggested different...How do you explain such differences?

- What do you think would happen if you did...?

Part IV
Practicing Listening

Task 1

Watch the video "Overcoming Fear of Asking Questions" and complete the following exercises.

1. **Watch the first part of the video titled "The Challenge" and fill in each blank with the information you hear from the video.**

   I think all college students experience some (1) _____ when

asking questions during class. I find that (2) _____ students often have additional (3) _____ to overcome. Many have been told since childhood, "Don't ask questions in (4) _____. It just makes you look (5) _____." In addition, many have a very low (6) _____ level. My (7) _____, therefore, was to find a way to let students know that asking questions, especially when they don't understand something, is an (8) _____ skill to become a successful, truly (9) _____ college learner. Without this skill, a student's ability to succeed in a course may be significantly (10) _____.

2. **Watch the second part of the video titled "Breakthrough Strategy" and match each approach listed in Column A to its effects on students that are listed in Column B.**

Column A: Approaches	Column B: Effects
1) Reposition the teacher as a personal guide to help students understand the subject without giving grades.	a. Students are told that there are no dumb questions and the questions they ask can also help with the learning of some other students who also have these questions.
2) Make students feel responsible for the learning of others.	b. Students are motivated to come up with some really insightful questions.
3) Use a lot of humor and a light touch in class.	c. Students are given a sense of permission to ask questions and get the help that they need.
4) Use the "Think, Pair, Share" format.	d. Students overcome a fear of having to ask their own questions as they are given time to share their questions with their partners.
5) Give students high praise for good questions.	e. Students feel relaxed in class and so they're intellectually ripe and open to critical thinking.

3. **Watch the last part of the video titled "Results" and list out the changes of the students.**

    1) Students gain _____.

    2) Students begin to _____.

    3) Students delve _____.

4) Students realize _____.

Task 2

Watch the video "How to Ask Questions at Academic Conferences and Seminar Presentations" to learn some suggestions made by a PhD student based on her own experience.

1. Take notes on the main points of the suggestions.

Suggestions	Main points of the suggestions	
Take really great notes during presentations.	• What to be written down	
	• Where to write the notes	
	• What to do with the notes	
	• What kind of questions to ask	
Be as supportive and as helpful as you can to a presenter.	• Attitude towards the presenters	
	• How to show disagreement	
Use the microphone if there's one provided.	• Why to use a microphone	
Share the air time during the question-and-answer period.	• What to do when no one asks a questions	
	• What to do when many people want to ask questions	

2. Decide whether the following statements are true (T) or false (F) according to the video.

1) It is necessary to take notes on key information and supporting details when listening in academic settings to prepare the questions that might be asked afterwards. (　　)

2) You are suggested to take a really respectful approach even when you find the speaker has said something deeply problematic. (　　)

3) Using a microphone when raising questions can help other participants to hear your questions better. 　　　　　　　　　　　(　)

4) You should wait to be the last to raise questions in order to show your courtesy. 　　　　　　　　　　　(　)

5) The more you attend, participate, listen, and observe at conferences or seminars, the easier it is to ask questions at these events. 　(　)

Task 3

Most of the time we ask questions for clarification. Watch the video made by Annemarie to learn when and how we can ask clarifying questions.

1. **Get the details of the four scenarios where people need clarification.**
   Scenario One: when ＿＿＿＿＿＿＿＿＿＿＿＿＿＿＿＿＿＿＿＿.
   The speaker: begins to ＿＿＿＿ to a question and ＿＿＿＿ a variety of details.
   The audience: don't know which side of the ＿＿＿＿＿ the speaker is on or what the ＿＿＿＿＿ really is.
   Solution: to ＿＿＿＿ what you heard and ＿＿＿＿ your understanding.

   Scenario Two: when ＿＿＿＿＿＿＿＿＿＿＿＿＿＿＿＿＿＿＿＿.
   The speaker: lacks connection in his or her speaking.
   The audience: feel ＿＿＿＿＿.
   Solution: to ask the speaker to ＿＿＿＿＿＿＿＿＿＿＿＿＿＿＿＿＿＿.

   Scenario Three: when ＿＿＿＿＿＿＿＿＿＿＿＿＿＿＿＿＿＿＿.
   The speaker's: opinion or idea is really ＿＿＿＿, lacks ＿＿＿＿＿.
   The audience: become ＿＿＿＿ or even ＿＿＿＿.
   Solution: to ask the speaker to provide something more ＿＿＿＿.

   Scenario Four: when ＿＿＿＿＿＿＿＿＿＿＿＿＿＿＿＿＿＿＿.
   The speaker: talks about something that is ＿＿＿＿＿ to you though the speaking is clear.
   The audience: can't understand certain vocabulary or topic.
   Solution: to tell the speaker your problem and ask for ＿＿＿＿.

2. **Link the following 13 questions to the appropriate scenarios.**
   1) If I understood you correctly, you're saying that [paraphrase opinion]. Am I correct?

2) I'd like to understand your thoughts further. Could you tell me more about...?

3) I didn't really catch the main point. Can you tell me how these two things are connected?

4) Just to clarify, what does [word or phrase] mean?

5) You made an interesting point about...Do you believe that [paraphrase opinion]?

6) Those are some interesting points. Could you expand on the details?

7) Sorry, I'm not so familiar with [topic]. Could you tell me more about it?

8) Could you explain how A and B are related to each other?

9) It sounds like you disagree/agree with [insert statement], is that right?

10) I apologize; I haven't heard that word "..." before. Could you tell me what you mean by [repeat phrase]?

11) I like your ideas. Could you give me more details on...?

12) Can I ask for some clarification? Would you mind explaining how A is connected to B?

13) To summarize, what you're saying is [paraphrase opinion], correct?

| Scenario One | Scenario Two | Scenario Three | Scenario Four |

Part V
Practicing Speaking

Task 1

Work in groups and exchange your previous experiences of asking questions at lectures, seminars, or conferences. Do you often ask questions in such settings? Why or why not? Have you been impressed by some questions raised by others in such settings?

Task 2

Work in groups and summarize what you have learnt from the videos you have watched in the previous part of Practicing Listening. How do you think these videos can help you to raise good questions in academic settings?

Part VI
Performing the Activity

Situation 1

Suppose you are going to attend an academic conference and prepare to raise questions in the Q&A session. Work in groups and make a list of the things that you can do to help you to raise a question appropriately and successfully in that setting.

Step 1: Divide the whole class into 4-member groups.

Step 2: Nominate each member in each group for one of the following roles: Facilitator, Timekeeper, Recorder, or Presenter.

Step 3: Students carry out the discussion and list out the things that can help to raise questions appropriately and successfully.

Step 4: Ask one group or two to present the results of their discussion.

Situation 2

Work in a group of four. One member makes a 3-minute presentation on a study he/she is doing or planning to do, and the other members take turns to raise a question based on the presentation. One turn ends when the presenter answers all the three questions, and then the next member takes the turn to make the presentation.

Step 1: Divide the whole class into groups with 4 members in each group.

Step 2: Student 1 makes a 3-minute presentation on a study he/she is doing or planning to do.

Step 3: Student 2, Student 3, and Student 4 ask Student 1 a question in turn.

Step 4: Student 2, Student 3, and Student 4 make a 3-minute presentation and then answer the three questions raised by the other members in turn.

 Exercises

 Task 1

Watch a video clip of the Q&A session in the Human-Computer Interaction Seminar, and take notes on how the question is asked.

1. **Complete what the questioner said with the information you hear from the video.**

    Great (1) _____. I was wondering, as you were talking in the leader part of the talking towards the future, one of the things that you were talking about were (2) _____. And I'm (3) _____, you know, to me, it (4) _____ a lot with patterns and design patterns, and I feel like, you know, one of the techniques that we have now is just collecting those patterns and also creating pattern languages. And so I'm wondering, how do you see the (5) _____ between patterns and strategies and what are some exciting things that you're thinking about, moving beyond ways that we have of collecting these or helping people learn strategies?

2. **Work in groups and analyze how the question was asked.**

3. **Discuss in groups what you can learn from this example.**

 Task 2

It has been suggested in this unit that we ask specific questions instead of making statements. Watch the second seminar video clip and complete the following exercises.

1. **Decide whether the following statements are true (T) or false (F) according to the video.**

    1) The questioner stated the question first and then followed up with the motivation. ( )

    2) It is not appropriate to express the motivation when raising questions as it will take more time. ( )

3) Expressing the motivation when asking questions may help explain the intention behind the question. (   )

4) It's better to express the motivation after the question as the motivation is not the focus. (   )

2.   **Discuss within a group on whether the questioner in this example asked his question successfully or not. Exchange your ideas with supporting explanations.**

Task 3

Watch the third seminar video clip to see what can be done when a questioner fails to raise a question clearly.

1.   **Choose the correct answer for each of the following questions according to the video.**

1) Which of the following may NOT be the reason to explain why the lecturer asked the questioner to restate his question?

A. The questioner used some technical terms that the lecturer couldn't understand.

B. The questioner didn't give enough details to help explain what he really wanted to say.

C. The questioner didn't express his thoughts elaborately.

D. Some of the words were not articulated clearly.

2) The questioner improved his question by _____.

A. asking a different question

B. raising his voices to repeat the same question

C. giving an example to help explain his question

D. rephrasing his question

2.   **Discuss in groups what you would do if you were the questioner and what you could do to help avoid such problems.**

Task 4

Watch the beginning part of the seminar video "Learning to Code: Why We Fail, How We Flourish". Suppose you were the audience in the seminar. Practice raising questions in the Q&A session.

1. **Watch the video clip and fill in the blanks in the table below with the information being mentioned in the clip.**

Presentation content	Details
Self-introduction	• Topic of the lecture: _____ • Name of the lecturer: _____ • Background of the lecturer: _____
Perspective to start with in his work	• Importance of learning code: _____ • Learning barriers: _____
Skills are more powerful than tools	• Tools only _____ skills. • Skills come from _____. • Learning comes from _____. • As a result, the lecturer spent most of his time teaching skills.
The first question to ask: Are people learning?	• Evidence: 1) Puzzles completed by Code.org's K-12 learners: _____ 2) Enrollment in AP CS: _____ 3) College: _____ 4) The 95 U.S. coding bootcamps in 2017: _____ 5) Employers: _____

2. **Discuss within groups on the content of this video clip and the questions the lecturer might receive. Exchange understandings with each other.**

Task 5

Watch a video clip of an interview to Sri M at the Youth Conference in 2018 and practice raising questions in similar settings.

1. **Watch the first part of the video clip and take notes on what Sri M said about the importance of education. Fill in each blank with an appropriate word from the list given below.**

    I think education is not just (1) _____. Information is easy. You don't even have to go to school now. You have Google, the new God "G" with capital. You don't have to go anywhere. But information is not enough. Information is useful. It's a (2) _____, like technology. But technology is based on (3) _____ science that turns into technology when it becomes useful to human beings. Then education is to be able to bring about, to make the young minds (4) _____. You can still collect a lot of technology in a brain. But the brain should remain open, open to (5) _____. Your heart pumps blood, of course, but it's the brain that takes. So can we try to bring about a change in the (6) _____ understanding, where we know that you can use information but use it for the good of (7) _____? Take nuclear energy for example. You can use nuclear energy for electricity. You can do it for (8) _____, but in wrong hands it can be very dangerous. So when you say education, it means to understand right, how to (9) _____, how to live, to understand humanity, to actually make your mind (10) _____. Creativity is not information. Creativity is to be able to blossom forward, pass from the old to the new, with respect to the old. I think that should be the kind of education that we need today.

A. creative	F. inner	L. tool
B. technology	G. perform	M. blossom
C. pure	H. humanity	N. professor
D. receive	I. respect	O. information
E. career	K. fancy	P. impression

2. **Watch the Q&A-with-the-audience session and discuss the following questions in groups.**

    1) What is the question raised by the audience?

    2) Why did Sri M ask the audience to clarify the question?

    3) What can we learn from this example?

📖 Project

The whole class will simulate a symposium. The class will be divided into groups of four members. Each group will first give a 10-minute presentation based on a study either done by its members or published in an academic journal, and then answer questions from other groups. When one group finishes the presentation, all the other groups will prepare at least two questions in 1 minute. For each presentation Q&A, only one group will be invited by the teacher to raise two questions. Each group uses the following rubric to rate other groups' questions in every category on a scale of 1 to 3.

Rubric for Raising Questions

	1	2	3
Subject Relevance	The student raises questions that are not related to the talk or even the subject.	The student raises questions that are related to the subject of the talk but not the talk itself.	The student raises questions that are closely related to the talk.
Delivery	The questions raised by the student can't be understood by the speaker due to the poor pronunciation or inappropriate language of the student.	The questions raised by the student can partly be understood by the speaker due to some mistakes in the pronunciation or the language of the student.	The questions raised by the student can be understood easily by the speaker due to the appropriate pronunciation and language of the student.
Physicality	The student has too much or too little body movement. The student displays little eye contact or facial expressions.	The student uses appropriate body movement and makes regular eye contact with the speaker.	The student customizes body movement and gestures that help with the delivery of the questions. The student engages the speaker with varied and compelling eye contact and facial expressions.

(Continued)

Politeness	The student raises questions in a rather rude manner, such as yelling at the speaker or using impolite language.	The student raises questions in a rather indifferent manner.	The student raises questions in a polite manner.

Scoring Sheet for Raising Questions

Group	Subject Relevance	Delivery	Physicality	Politeness	Total Score
1					
2					
3					
4					
...					

Unit 7

Chairing a Session

Part I
Introducing the Unit

Session chairs play an important role in conferences or seminars. They are expected to draw out session themes, create inclusive environments, handle unexpected situations, and ensure that sessions run smoothly. Their duties may vary slightly at different kinds of sessions, but all the chairpersons share some common responsibilities.

Session chairs are usually appointed because of their expertise in the topic of the session. If you get a chance to chair a session, take it as an honor and you will soon find it a rewarding job. In this unit, you will learn the general duties of chairs, and see examples of chairing different kinds of sessions. You will get ready to be an effective chair.

Part II
Learning about the Activity

A conference usually includes many different sessions, for example, the opening and closing ceremonies, the plenary session, paper presentation sessions, panel discussion sessions, poster sessions, workshops, etc. Chairing different sessions may involve different tasks, but generally the chairs take the role of an organizer, a coordinator, and a facilitator. To chair a session successfully, you need to prepare for it carefully.

→ General duties

A chairperson usually has such duties as opening a session, introducing speakers, managing the time, moderating the Q&A or discussion, and wrapping up the session.

❶ Opening a session

In most cases, it is the chairperson who announces the opening of a session or a conference. There are different ways to open a session. The chairperson may start with a very brief self-introduction or with thanks to the organizer, special guests and sponsors. But most importantly, when opening a session, the chairperson needs to introduce the theme of the session, and how the session is going to proceed.

The theme of the session must be well presented in the title of the session. The chairperson can also describe briefly the background of the concerning issue, its significance, and how it fits into the overall conference. Ideally, the topics of the session's presentations are previewed in the right sequence, which shows the internal logic of the session.

After announcing the theme of the session, it is also necessary for the chairperson to inform the audience of how the session is to take place. This includes, for instance, how long the session will be, whether there will be a break, how many speakers there will be, how the questions will be taken, etc. Also, requirements such as muting the mobile phones should be noted.

❷ Introducing speakers

Introducing a speaker is much more than reading aloud his/her name and presentation title. Of course, a chairperson does need to pronounce the speaker's name loudly and correctly, but do not stop there. Place the speaker in context, for example, which research group or institution the speaker comes from, what degrees or positions he/she holds from what universities or organizations, what his/her research interests are, and what achievements or latest developments he/she has made. In doing so, the audience's attention can be aroused, and the speaker's prestige built up.

Sometimes, if the chairperson knows the speaker personally, it may be appropriate to mention an anecdote that shows the speaker in a positive but different light. If kept short and good-humored, such stories will help break the ice and bring the speaker closer to the audience.

❸ Managing the time

Perhaps the most important task of the chairperson is to manage the time well, so that the session ends on time, and each speaker has an equal amount of time.

This is never an easy task. Very often, speakers plan to include too much information, and the audience have too many questions. To prevent this from happening, the chair needs to inform the speakers before the session of their time limit, and communicate with them on the timing signals. There are various ways to give timing signals. For example, to indicate that two minutes is left, you can raise your hand, or show a paper sign, or say "two minutes left", or simply stand up and walk towards the podium. If the time is running out and speakers continue, press them to wrap up. If it does not work, the chair needs to stop them politely to guarantee the time for other speakers. It is unpleasant to interrupt people, but it is the job that the chairperson must do.

If the audience have a lot of questions, or one question triggers a heated debate, the chairperson is supposed to choose only a few questions, or stop the ongoing discussion. This can be done by encouraging the audience to continue a private conversation with the speaker later during the coffee break.

❹ Moderating the Q&A/discussion

When there is time for the Q&A, the session chair should first make clear the ground rules, such as the number of questions expected and the time allotted. Then the chair is responsible for encouraging the questions, and including questions from as many attendees as possible. He/she can designate the questioner, or let the speakers manage the questions themselves. But in either way, he/she should be a timekeeper as described above.

In some discussion panels, the chairperson may take the role of a moderator as well when there is not one. In that case, the chair prepares a list of questions for the panelists, and makes comments on the discussion.

❺ Wrapping up the session

There are usually three steps to close the session. First, the theme of the session or conference is restated. The chairperson may recap the major messages of the presentations, or draw an overall conclusion. Then, thanks are given to the speakers, the audience, the organizer, and sponsors. Sometimes, gratitude can also be expressed in the opening of the session. Finally, practical information is provided to the audience on what is coming next, such as where the coffee break takes place, when the next session begins, and how the feedback is submitted.

→ Tips for success

Here are five tips to help you become a successful chair.

❶ Be prepared

Prepare your role as a chair. You need to get familiar with the names of the presenters and their abstracts at your session. Do some research on the speakers so that you can introduce them accurately. Contact the speakers in advance either at the conference before the session or via email, to check if they will show up and their presentation topics are unchanged. Make sure they know the time limit and timing signals. To ensure that the session will run smoothly, come to the meeting room early and get the presentation slides preloaded. It would be better if you know how to contact IT support in case anything goes wrong.

❷ Be inclusive

Some speakers might be more prominent than others, but introduce their publications and achievements equally, and ensure a fair share of the session for each speaker. Make sure that every speaker gets at least one comment or question. Prepare one question for each speaker in case there is a long silence in the Q&A process. But if there are too many questions for a speaker, do not hog the time.

❸ Be selfless

As a session chair, do not steal the thunder of the speakers in your session. Remember that you are not a "sage on the stage". Keep stories about your own research to the coffee time, and leave the stage for the speakers. If you have questions or comments on the speakers' research, talk to them later. Give the audience more time to ask questions.

❹ Be attentive

During the presentations, listen attentively and take notes on points that could be used for comments or questions later. When it is time for questions, make eye contact with those who raise their hands so they know you have seen them.

❺ Be firm

When it comes to keeping time, you should be firm. It might be unpleasant to stop a speaker from talking, or an audience member from asking questions, but when time is running out, that is the right thing for the chair to do.

Make sure you remind the speakers in advance of their time limit and your timing signs, and be prepared to stop those who use up their time even if they are of higher academic ranks. Also be strict with the audience. Stop the second question from the same person to create opportunities for others, and cut off more questions when it is about to fall behind schedule.

Part III
Learning Useful Expressions

→ Opening a session

- Hello everybody and welcome.

- First of all, I'd like to welcome everybody and thank you all for coming to today's meeting.

- This session is on...The first two presentations will report on...Then the remaining three presentations will show...

- The purpose/aim/objective of this session is...

- In this session, we'll focus on...

→ Introducing speakers

- Before we get started, let me introduce...

- I'd like you all to meet...

- Our first speaker today is...Our next speaker is...He graduated from...University, and he is now conducting research on...at...University.

- Unfortunately, Professor Li can't join us today—he sends his apologies.

- I'd like to apologize on behalf of Mr. Li. He can't be with us today due to...

→ Managing the time

- Can you please come to your conclusion? There is only one minute left.

- You've got...minutes each for your talk, and then...minutes for questions. I'm going to interrupt you about a minute before your talk finishes.

- Your time is up. I must ask you to stop.

- I'm sorry, but I have to stop you there, because we are running out of time / because we need to stick to the schedule.

→ Moderating the Q&A/discussion

- Now we've got...minutes for questions.

- Come on. Who is courageous enough to ask the first question?

- What exactly do you mean by...?

- We are running out of the time, so let's move on.

- Sorry, thank you for the questions, but we need to give other attendees a chance to ask questions, too.

- I'm afraid we don't have time for further discussion now. Maybe we can discuss about it later in the coffee break.

→ Wrapping up the session

- When we kick off today and start to think about what we've achieved out of the day, ...

- I'd like to extend a special thank you to... / I'd like to thank/acknowledge...

- I'm grateful for the support of... / I'd like to express my sincere gratitude to...

- If you are interested in..., then do not miss the afternoon session on...

- I hope to see many of you at our awards ceremony this afternoon.

- If you've got any great ideas about how we can do things better, we'd like to hear from you.

Part IV
Practicing Listening

 Task 1

The video introduces how to CHAIR an academic session. Watch the video TWICE, and answer the questions.

1. **What does each of the five letters in the word CHAIR signify?**

    C: _____

    H: _____

    A: _____

    I: _____

    R: _____

2. **What did the chairman say to open the session?**

    _____

3. **How long did the chairman give each speaker for his/her talk, and for the questions?**

    _____

4. **When did the chairman plan to warn the speaker of the time limit, and when to stop the speaker?**

    _____

    _____

    _____

5. **How did the chairman warn the speaker of the time, and how did he stop the speaker?**

    _____

    _____

    _____

Task 2

Wibur K. Woo Greater China Business Conference, held annually by UCLA Anderson School of Management, aims to bring together today's business leaders, professionals, academics and students to discuss current business challenges and impact of the increasing role of the Greater China Business Association. This video presents the students' co-chairing of the opening of the 2018 Conference.

1. **Watch the video ONCE, and choose the right answers to the following questions.**

   1) Which of the following statements is CORRECT about the two student chairpersons?

      A. Both of them were full-time MBA students at UCLA Anderson.

      B. One of them was president of the Greater China Business Association.

      C. One of them was a second-year MBA student; the other was a third-year MBA student.

      D. Both of them were directors of the Center for Chinese Studies.

   2) The two chairpersons were in charge of different jobs when chairing. Jason's opening remarks included _____, while Longying was responsible for _____.

      A. self introduction

      B. an introduction to the topics of the conference

      C. an introduction to the first speaker

      D. an introduction to the different sessions of the conference

      E. expressing thanks to the concerning people and organizations

   3) Whom did the chairperson acknowledge?

      A. the guests

      B. the moderators

      C. the past student conference directors

      D. sponsors

      E. conference organizers

      F. China General Chamber of Commerce New York

      G. the UCLA Asia Pacific Center

      H. the Center for Management Studies

      I. the Woo family

   4) Which of the following was NOT one of the sponsors of the conference?

      A. PWC and Cathay Bank

      B. Lancea

      C. Bronze

      D. Cox Castle & Nicolson

5) Which of the following was NOT one of the conference organizers?

　　A. the UCLA Anderson's Center for Global Management

　　B. the UCLA Anderson's Greater China Business Association

　　C. the UCLA Chinese Students and Scholars Association

　　D. the UCLA Asia Pacific Center

2. **Watch the first chairperson's opening part again, and write down what the business leaders would talk about at the conference.**

　　_____

　　_____

　　_____

3. **Watch the first chairperson's acknowledgements again, and write down all the expressions he used to show gratitude.**

　　_____

　　_____

　　_____

4. **Watch the introduction to Judy Olian again, and fill in each blank with NO MORE THAN FOUR words.**

Judy Olian, (1) _____ and John E. Anderson Chair in Management at UCLA Anderson. Dean Olian has been (2) _____ of the conference over the years. Since her appointment in 2006, she has greatly (3) _____ UCLA Anderson's focus on international business and (4) _____, developed (5) _____ with an emphasis in Asia, particularly the Greater China region, and advanced and strengthened UCLA Anderson into one of the (6) _____ in the world with a truly global focus. It was also under Dean Olian's leadership that the Center for Global Management was established here at UCLA Anderson.

Task 3

This video presents how the chairperson closed the Power of Innovation Symposium.

1. **Watch the video ONCE, and answer the following questions.**

　　1) What steps are involved in the closing remarks?

　　_____

_____

_____

2) Since the theme of the symposium was the Power of Innovation, what did the chairperson call on the people to do after the symposium?

_____

_____

_____

3) Who did the chairperson thank?

_____

_____

_____

2. **Watch the last part of the closing remark again, and fill in each blank with NO MORE THAN THREE words.**

We've received lots of (1) _____ from people about the benefits to live they felt during the course of hearing things and being a part of today's (2) _____. We'd like to build on it for (3) _____. So if you've got any great ideas about how we can do things better or the things that we should cover, we'd love to (4) _____ you about those ideas so that can make next year's program even better. And for those of you who (5) _____ the awards process tonight, good luck and I hope you have success.

Part V
Practicing Speaking

 Task 1

Watch a short video on the roles of the chairperson. Then work in pairs, and discuss the

roles that a chairperson plays. You can first share the information you hear from the video, and then give your own opinion on the chairman's roles that are not mentioned in the video.

Task 2

Work in pairs. If you have chaired an academic conference, session or seminar, share with your partner your experience. If not, describe a chairperson who left deep impression on you. Then discuss together on what makes a good chairperson.

Task 3

Watch again the last part of the Task 2 video in Practicing Listening, learn from it, and practice introducing the speakers. Suppose you would chair a symposium held by your school, and the dean of your school would be the first keynote speaker. Do some research on your dean, and write a short draft introducing him/her as the first speaker. Then present it to your classmates.

Part VI
Performing the Activity

Situation 1

The following chart shows part of the agenda of MIT Sloan Conference on Aug 29, 2015, with the theme of Growth Opportunities in Latin America and China. Imagine you would chair Panel 2. Prepare the beginning and the ending parts of your chairing. In the beginning part, please introduce the topic of the session, the presenters, and necessary requirements. In the ending part, please show your gratitude, and remind the audience of what comes next. Work in groups, present your chairing in the group, and select the best chair in your group.

9:45–11:15	**Panel 2: Growth Prospects in China** Sustained growth in China is critical both domestically and internationally. Slowing growth and lending rates combined with high debt have raised questions, but how concerned should business and policy leaders be? **Presenters:** **Yasheng Huang**, MIT Sloan School of Management, USA **Sun Pei**, Fudan University, School of Management, China **Chong-en Bai**, School of Economics and Management of Tsinghua University, China **Xinzhong Xu**, Lingnan (University) College, Sun Yat-sen University, China **Jian Gao**, China Development Bank, China
11:15–11:45	**Lunch Break**
11:45–12:45	**Lunch Speakers:** **André Loes**, HSBC Latin America, Brazil **Paul Mackel**, HSBC Hong Kong, China
12:45–13:00	**Break**

Step 1: Divide the class into groups of four or five student.

Step 2: Half the groups prepare the beginning part of the chairing, and the other half prepare the ending part of the chairing.

Step 3: Each student takes turns to present his/her chairing in the group.

Step 4: Select the best chair in the group.

Step 5: The best chairs present their chairing in front of the whole class.

Situation 2

Suppose you are one of the chairs at the Annual International AIDS Conference. Your job is to acknowledge the concerning bodies and people in the closing ceremony. The conference is organized by the International AIDS Society in partnership with UNAIDS and regional and local partners such as EACS (European AIDS Clinical Society) and Ministry of Foreign Affairs. Also, the following graph shows the conference sponsors and supporters. Try to give thanks by using a variety of expressions as shown below.

Conference sponsors & supporters

The conference organizers gratefully acknowledge the generous support provided by the following:

Major industry sponsors

 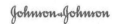  

Corporate sponsors

Platinum	Silver	Bronze

Media partners

  THE LANCET

Donors

- I would like to thank...
- I would like to acknowledge...
- I would like to extend a special thank-you to...
- I would also like to thank and recognize...
- We thank...for their support and commitment to the conference.
- We are also grateful for the support of...

Exercises

Task 1

This video clip shows the chair's introduction to DUG conference.

1. **Watch the video TWICE, take notes and fill in the blanks with the information you hear.**

Audience	The conference brings a variety of _____ and companies together including _____ and specially invited guests from the _____ and universities.
Housekeeping skills	She showed the audience the fire exits. She asked everybody to _____ _____. All the presentations will be available on _____.
Topic	The topic for this year is "How _____ _____, —visualizing, distilling and _____". The topic has been promoted by the _____, and members had various discussions about the recent developments, availability and _____ _____.
Sponsor	The event is sponsored and supported by _____ _____.
Speakers	The details and biographies of the speakers are _____ _____.
Special arrangement	This year's Master's Projects from the _____ Center will be outside during _____. A workshop session will be _____ so the audience will have energy for it. This session seeks to identify ___ _____.

2.   **What did the chair suggest the attendees do if they have any thoughts or questions?**

_____

_____

Task 2

In this video, Russell Climie from Grand Rapids gives some tips to event organizers on how to help their MCs (Master of Ceremony) better introduce keynote speakers.

1.   **Watch the video ONCE, and answer the following questions.**

1) What are the three tips given by Russell?

_____

_____

_____

2) What does Russell mean by the first tip?

_____

_____

_____

3) Why does Russell think that the third tip is important?

_____

_____

_____

2.   **Watch the speaker's second tip again, and fill in the blanks with the information you hear.**

For example, if we were at an event for school administrators or something like that, and Jerry Smith was coming up, and he was a (1) _____,
I would say something like this. "Folks, I'm really (2) _____ to introduce our speaker this afternoon. He comes from a background of being a (3) _____ at a large school district, and then moved on to create (4) _____ that now works with dozens and dozens of districts across the country that not only help improve (5) _____
_____ but also (6) _____

_____. We brought him out today to speak to you because of the results he has provided and created in other scenarios and that's (7) _____ _____. So without further ado, help me (8) _____ Jerry Smith."

Task 3

In this video, a voice coach gives you some tips on how to sound confidently and make a good impression when chairing a meeting.

1. **Watch the video ONCE, and answer the following questions.**

   1) The voice coach compared chairing a meeting to being the pilot of a plane. What is the similarity between the two?

   _____

   _____

   2) The voice coach thought the advice given by John Wayne was essential to chairing a meeting. What is it? Do you think it also works when chairing an academic meeting?

   _____

   _____

2. **Watch the video again, and fill in the blanks to complete the details in the table below.**

You need to sit well.	You need to _____ in your chair. You need to get your sit bones and your tailbone glued down in your chair so that you can _____ and _____. You need to have a long straight spine. No _____. You need to have your shoulders _____ so that you seem _____.
You also need to be really _____.	You need to have a clear _____, and you need to know exactly _____. You've got to _____, so you know exactly how long each section is going to take. You need to make sure that _____ _____, which means you have to be able to _____ _____.

(Continued)

You need to think about _____.	You want your voice not to be too _____.
	You want your voice to be in your gut because that gives you a more _____ tone.
	A trick to make your voice lower is to _____.

Task 4

In the video, Yasheng Huang, international program professor in Chinese economy and business at MIT Sloan, delivered the closing remarks of MIT Sloan Latin America–China Conference in 2014.

1. **Watch the video ONCE, and write down the main ideas expressed in the closing remarks.**

    _____

    _____

    _____

2. **Watch the video again, and choose the right answer to each of the following questions.**

    1) Which of the following statements is NOT correct about the conference?

       A. The conference was on Friday.

       B. The conference was held in Brazil.

       C. The conference was a second conference on Latin America and China.

       D. The discussions at the conference ranged from macroeconomics to movies, film stars, food and soccer.

    2) What did Professor Huang mean by "we end the conference on a very high note"?

       A. The conference ends with a musical.

       B. The conference ends with something cultural.

       C. The conference ends with something unexpected.

       D. The conference ends with sincere thanks.

    3) Which of the following was NOT thanked by Professor Huang?

       A. Sponsors.

       B. Colleagues.

       C. Magazines.

D. Students.

E. Panelists.

3. **Professor Huang thanked many people for their contributions. Please match the names of the people with what they had done.**

1) David Capilouto   a) master of ceremony and conceptualizer of many ideas

2) Steward   b) worked so hard on this conference from the very beginning

3) Julie Strong   c) handled logistics and got a visa for Professor Huang

4) Angie Brown   d) handled difficult challenges and made life easier

5) San Renee   e) made connections to Latin American business and academic communities

 Task 5

This video clip is taken from a panel discussion in Wilbur K. Woo Greater China Business Conference on the topic "Embracing Innovation to Shape the Path". The session was moderated by Christopher Tang, who was a UCLA professor and holder of Edward W. Carter Chair in Business Administration.

1. **Watch the video ONCE, and fill in the blanks in the table below with the information you hear.**

Jeff Moran	He is now the _____ of International Vitamin Corporation (IVC).
	He used to be a _____ at DTT, an industry-leading technology-based _____ company.
	He served as _____ and chief financial officer of SIN Energy, an international energy management _____ _____ company.
	He has a Master of Management degree in _____ from the Kellogg School of Management and Northwestern University as well as a _____ degree from the University of Minnesota.

(Continued)

Xiaohui Xu	He has been the _____ of COMAC, Commercial Aircraft Corporations of China, since 2013, responsible for the shareholder relationships, _____, and _____. He used to be a director of COMAC's general office in Shanghai where he was responsible for _____ with the public, government, and suppliers. From 2005 to 2008, he was the _____ of the Beijing organizing committee for the _____ in 2008. He was previously a _____ for Xinhua News Agency.
Brendan Riley	He's the _____ of the fleet sales of BYD Motors Incorporated. He joined BYD in 2012 with over _____ years of experience in the area of business development, _____ _____, and operations. He used to run the BYD_____ sales to the Long Beach public transit company. Before that, he served as the vice president of _____ at PTB Sales in Azusa, California. He served _____ terms as the _____ of Southern California Chapter of AVS for science and technology. He received his _____ degree from the University of San Tommaso. He can speak two languages fluently, English and _____. He has won _____ and holds a helicopter and multi-engine instruments _____.

2.　**Watch the video again, and answer the following questions.**

1) What are the questions asked by the moderator to the panelists?

_____

_____

_____

2) What are the moderator's comments on the discussion at the end of the clip? And what do you predict will follow? Share your prediction with your partner.

Comments: _____

_____

_____

Prediction: _____

3. **The job of a moderator in a discussion panel session is slightly different from that of a chair in a presentation session. Work with your partner, and discuss on the similarities and differences between the two.**

Project

Work in groups. Suppose your school is holding an international conference, and you are invited to chair the conference. You may first look for some conference samples in your field. Take turns to chair the presentation of your group members.

Unit 8

Socializing at
Academic Events

Part I
Introducing the Unit

Attending an academic event such as a conference is a great opportunity to meet new people in your research field. However, it might be difficult for first-time conference attendees. They would find it difficult to get to know people and to mingle with them. This is especially true to introvert people who fear making a fool of themselves in front of others and those who do not really aim to socialize and make friends.

In this unit, we are going to present the five WH's and one How about socializing at academic events, namely, why, when, where and who to socialize, how to socialize and what to say. Then you will see some examples of networking at both academic and non-academic events. You can learn some useful strategies from them, and then put the strategies into practice.

Part II

Learning about the Activity

➜ Why

As mentioned previously, attending academic events is a great opportunity for you to meet new people in your field and do some networking. A large network will be helpful to secure new projects, collaborations or jobs to progress in your academic career. Besides, being alone at the event is no good to alleviate your social anxiety or increase your confidence. So why not go out of your comfort zone and try to bond with others?

➜ When and where

You actually have a lot to do before, during and after any academic event.

Before the event, you can do some homework. Your social success should not depend just on your personal skills. Planning ahead is a key. You can know who will attend the conference and decide if you want to meet them. As many conferences nowadays will create the LinkedIn event, a group email or a WeChat group of the conference, it will be easy for you to locate the people you want to meet. You can directly contact some of the attendees via LinkedIn or WeChat. Writing an email is a more formal way to contact. You can email them and say who you are, what research you are doing, and ask whether they would have time for a cup of coffee to discuss ideas or anything else. It helps if you are also presenting a paper. This way you will get yourself known.

During the conference, there are surely many chances for you to socialize, for instance, between the talks, after a talk, at the conference dinner, and at coffee breaks. In fact, some idle moments can also be a great opportunity to socialize, such as standing in the queue for coffee, sitting around electricity outlets to recharge your gadgets, or waiting for the next speaker. If there is a poster session, that is also a great chance to meet and talk. People with posters are often standing there wishing somebody would come over and ask about their work. They will be eager to talk to you about it.

After the event, you may also get to know new people when you are on your return home. Many international conferences have been in places with small airports, so many conference attendees are waiting for the same flights. Train station is also a good place to socialize if the conference is national and the attendees are from different parts of the country. When you get home, you can also contact your new friends from the academic event as soon as possible so that you will be fresh in their minds. You can write an email or contact them via LinkedIn or WeChat, asking follow-up questions or saying "Thank you" for what they have done for you.

→ Who

Meeting new people is key to expanding your network. But who should you talk to?

If you feel attracted by the charisma of big professors in your field, go ahead and raise questions to them or approach them after their talks. Talking with them can be really rewarding experiences.

Unfortunately however, reputed scholars have a busy agenda and they tend to talk to peers of the same academic rank. Then you have the young scholars. They are of your same age, more open-minded, with smaller egos and with fewer people to talk to. You can also use this chance to meet other graduate students. Your graduate student peers will be your community in the field: these are the people who are at a stage similar to you and who will be willing to plow through rough drafts of your work, and to share happiness and sorrows of student life.

→ How and what

❶ Prepare two versions of elevator pitches

An elevator pitch is a quick summary of yourself. It is named for the amount of time it usually takes to deliver it—the duration of a short elevator ride (about 30 to 60 seconds or 75 words).

It will be convenient to prepare an elevator pitch in advance when people ask things about you. It can include what you do, why and how you do it. You can even have two versions ready, depending on who is asking. One version is used for non-experts with plain language, and the other for experts in your field, with all sorts of complicated jargon as being scientifically correct.

❷　Ask more, listen more, and talk less about yourself

The goal of networking is getting people to like you. And the key to this is to ask more, listen more, and talk less about yourself. People will not like you if you keep talking about yourself. If you show a genuine interest in another person, let him/her do the talking and when he/she stops, keep him/her talking by asking follow-up questions. By so doing, you will make him/her feel important and worth listening to.

❸　Don't only talk about work

After a long day of academic events, it might be more relaxing to talk about something else. Try to shift conversations towards non-work related topics like hobbies and anecdotes. This is also called making small talks. You can ask people what they like the most about their job or school, or what they like doing when they are free. If they mention something in passing that seems to be interesting to them, ask more about that. If you want to show your sincerity instead of just being polite, you can ask for specific details. However, if you start by making a small talk, but you do not want to dwell on it, you can try to make a smooth transition to your intended topic.

❹　Talk about academic topics

If you want to get some help or to progress academically, this is definitely the topic you want to dwell on. You can gradually transition to their research interest, the study they are doing right now, the difficulties they meet on the way, and how they find their solutions. Remember, the key here is not to demonstrate your knowledge and good judgment, but to seek common ground and opportunity for future cooperation. Therefore, you do not need to be too critical here.

❺　Share about yourself

Only asking questions makes you sound like an interrogator. You also need to share some information about yourself. This kind of back-and-forth conversation makes people bond. You may come up with something to relate to after the others finish talking, or ask them a related question after you have made your statement. For example, if you are talking about academic topics, after the others finish talking about their difficulties in research, you can share your similar problems in the research process, and offer some possible solutions suggested by your supervisor or other experts for their reference. They may be enlightened and feel grateful to you.

After knowing all these, you may still feel nervous about socializing in academic events. That is normal. Even if you fail, you can still try again and again. If you do come across someone who does not feel like talking, then you know why he is not mixing, and you move along. Everyone you talk to, as a rule, increases your confidence and comfort. If you are persistent, humble, friendly, and willing to learn, you will eventually break through.

Part III
Learning Useful Expressions

→ Knowing people for the first time

- Hi! I don't think we've met—I'm...

- Hi, nice meeting you! I'm...

- How do you know people here?

- Where are you from?

- What made you choose to study this subject?

- This is my first conference.

- I'm new to the field.

- Can I ask what the...group at...University focuses on?

- Oh, you're from...University?

- Oh, you're the guy/girl with that...paper, right?

- So, what do you do?

- What are you working on?

→ Making small talks

- How are things?

- How have you been?

- How is your day so far?

- Any plans for the weekend/tonight?

- What do you like the most about your job?

- What do you like doing when you don't work?

- You mention something about..., what...was that?

- What do you do more specifically?

- Wait, how does...actually work?

- Do you go to...often?

→ Asking follow-up questions

- What is your research about?

- Do you have some exciting results so far?

- How is it to do research in your group? Pros, cons?

- How is it to live in your city?

- What were the toughest moments in your PhD?

- What are your scientific plans?

➔ Sharing a little bit about yourself

- Yeah, I used to work in...as well and it was exhausting but I'm happy I did it.

- I love...My grandparents live close to the water in...so I was there often as a child, but I never learned to...because the waves aren't good there.

- I listen to a lot of...music. I want to go to this festival in...called...

➔ Postponing a conversation

- I am working on..., and I know that you are...; do you think you'll have time after today's schedule ends / tomorrow morning / at lunch break on Tuesday to sit down and talk for a while?

- Hi, I'm...from...I've always wanted to meet you. But now I'm in hurry to...Here is my card. Shall we talk sometime later?

➔ Asking for recommendation

- I have not gotten into...yet, but I still wanted to ask you...

- I have not gotten into...yet. Since you're an expert, would you mind recommending a good starting point? Like a survey, or a few key papers?

Part IV
Practicing Listening

Task 1

Watch the talk "How to Network at Academic Conferences" given by Dr. Amelia Aldao, a clinical psychologist, and complete the following exercises.

1. **Watch the video ONCE and write down the top 7 tips given by the speaker.**
    1) _____

2) _____

3) _____

4) _____

5) _____

6) _____

7) _____

2. **Watch the video again and decide whether the following statements are true (T) or false (F) according to the speaker's advice.**

   1) If you already have some connections, they do not need to be strengthened.

   ( )

   2) You do not need to talk to people who work in a completely different area from yours.   ( )

   3) Poster sessions and special interest groups are both great chances to meet people.   ( )

   4) If you stay in the center of the action, you will give people the impression of being self-important.   ( )

   5) If you want to hang out with some friends in town, make good use of the time during the conferences such as skipping some unimportant sessions.

   ( )

   6) If you are interested in the city where the conference is held, you may extend your stay by a day or two instead of using the conference time for tourism.

   ( )

   7) When you meet people at conferences, you should stay positive by focusing on what you like about their work in order to find common ground for possible collaboration.   ( )

   8) When the conference is over, you should stop connecting with your new friends until the next conference is around the corner.   ( )

Task 2

The following two excerpts are from the lecture "How to Prepare for an Academic Conference—10 Essential Tips" by Dr. Jay Phoenix Singh. Watch the videos and complete the following exercises.

1. **Watch the first excerpt "Print Copies of Your Resume" ONCE and fill each blank with one word based on the information you have heard.**

    If you are a student, (1) _____ along several print-out copies of your (2) _____ because you never know who you will meet at these conferences. Take himself for example: When he was an (3) _____ student, he went to a conference and met a professor from the University of Maryland whose work he (4) _____. Although the speaker had not done his preparation work and did not know who would be at the conference, he went up to the professor and (5) _____ on his work and on some related issues. The professor was deeply impressed, saying, "You know my (6) _____ stuff!" After that, the speaker introduced himself by saying that he was an undergraduate and was thinking about applying to the professor's university. Then the professor literally asked whether the speaker had any copies of his resume or a card, because he was open for (7) _____ at that time and he found that he and the speaker had a lot of common interest. So the speaker went out and printed out his resume and brought it back to the professor after (8) _____ him (9) _____. Therefore, the speaker suggested that the students can have several copies ready and put them in with the conference material. And this will increase the chance of getting a job or a master's or doctoral (10) _____.

2. **Watch the second clip "Dress and Act Professionally Whilst Travelling" ONCE and choose the best answer to each question.**

    1) It's important to dress and act professionally when ____.
        A. you are at the conferences
        B. you are on the plane there or back
        C. you are in a taxi waiting line
        D. All of the above.

2) Why does the speaker say he can maintain a long-term friendly relationship with the lady he met on a subway ride?

A. Because he was a friendly person.

B. Because he was dressed nice and acted properly when they first met.

C. Because he became a really big player in his field.

D. All of the above.

Task 3

Conference dinner is also a good opportunity for you to socialize with people in your academic field. Then, what etiquette should you know in order to network with others with respect while enjoying your dinner? Watch a video on dinner etiquette and complete the following exercises.

1. **Watch the video ONCE and decide whether the following behaviors are appropriate or not. Tick the boxes beside the appropriate behaviors. Then watch the video again to check your answers.**

1) Whenever you are asked a question while interacting with others during a conference dinner, you will answer it immediately to show your respect.	
2) If you have food in your mouth when you are about to answer a question, you can finish the bite you are chewing before you give the response.	
3) Prior to asking someone a question, look at the person to make sure that he/she is not chewing with the mouth full.	
4) Take big bite sizes when you are not asked a question.	
5) Never judge the timing of asking a question.	
6) When dining on the same table, try to engage the persons on either side of you if they are not participating in a conversation.	
7) Even if it's a small table, only interact with the people on either side of you.	
8) Instead of pointing at the table, use an open-hand gesture.	
9) Show your interest in others' conversation via your eye contact, nodding of the head, etc.	

Part V
Practicing Speaking

Task 1

Work in groups and check on the Internet: What is Chinese dinner etiquette? Is there any difference between Chinese culture and Western culture as far as dining etiquette is concerned? Report your findings to the whole class.

Task 2

Imagine that you are in the middle of a conversation with a new acquaintance at an academic event. She has just talked about her research interest and her recent failure in publishing her research article. She would like to hear some advice from you. How will you respond? What follow-up questions will you ask her? What information will you share about yourself? Remember to maintain a positive attitude towards her. Then role-play the conversation with your pair-work partner.

Task 3

Watch a talk given by a public speaking coach entitled "Public Speaking Tips: Easy Networking Tip for Conferences". Think about another networking tip that you have tried, and introduce it to your pair-work partner by imitating the public speaking coach. Include some concrete examples to illustrate your point.

Task 4

Work in groups. Try to find two videos on the Internet or parts of a movie that contain one successful instance of networking at academic conferences and one unsuccessful instance. Observe carefully how people interact with each other and note down the strategies the speakers have used. Discuss with your group members about how you can incorporate these strategies into your own networking practice, and ways to avoid the wrong practices in the future.

Strategies of successful networking	Ways to incorporate these strategies

(Continued)

Wrong practices of unsuccessful networking	Ways to avoid them

Part VI
Performing the Activity

Situation 1

Suppose you are a graduate student and you are at a conference dinner. You try to sit down at a table with someone unfamiliar but of similar age. They turn out to be graduate students from different universities. Talk with them while having dinner.

Step 1: Divide the whole class into groups of four to five.

Step 2: Each member will take turns to be the new-comer to the dinner table.

Step 3: Initiate talks with other group members/ guests at the table.

Step 4: Hold a group discussion about the best practice to connect with people.

Step 5: Share the tips with the whole class.

Situation 2

The whole class simulates a poster session. Each student will print out an outline of a study. Then divide the whole class into two groups. The two groups will take turns to act as the poster presenters and the attendees. Try to focus on building connections with each other.

Step 1: Each student will print out an outline of a study, which should include the title of the research, some background information and need for the study, the research question(s), methodology and results.

Step 2: Divide the class into two groups. They will take turns to be the poster presenters and the attendees.

Step 3: The students will talk with each other during the poster session about the research and related topics. Find common ground. Think of possible directions in which you might cooperate in the future.

Step 4: Each student will keep a log on what they have gained through this practice.

📖 Exercises

Task 1

Watch a video entitled "Do's and Don'ts of Networking at Conferences" and complete the exercises.

1. **Read the following statements and judge which are Do's and which are Don'ts. Put a tick (√) next to each statement that is Do and a cross (×) to the statement that is Don't.**

   1) Make an entrance that looks sharp. ( )

   2) Be well groomed, smile and stand tall. ( )

   3) Head to a conference without preparing. ( )

   4) Research who the speakers are and what companies will be attending. ( )

   5) Be original in what you say to people. ( )

   6) Use the opportunity of asking questions to find out something interesting about the person. ( )

   7) Focus your time on talking to just one person. ( )

   8) Bring snacks and drinks until it's time to eat meals. ( )

   9) Spend a lot of time at the refreshment table. ( )

   10) Wear something distinguished so that you stand out. ( )

   11) Wear a signature tie, a smart jacket, a pair of good shoes, or anything that would be a great conversation. ( )

   12) Wear something that is very original and attracts everyone's attention. ( )

   13) Start a conversation asking people what they do for work and then immediately start pitching to them. (pitch: to present or advertise especially in a high-pressure way) ( )

   14) Focus on connecting with the right people and collecting their cards. ( )

   15) Write small personal notes on the back to help you remember that person. ( )

16) Hand your business cards out to everyone that you see.   (   )

2.   **Since this video is targeted at people attending business networking conferences, some tips may not fit other settings. Decide which of the above Do's are unnecessary for academic conferences. And why?**

_____

_____

_____

Task 2

When you are socializing in academic events, you can make small talk with new acquaintances to build rapport. But sooner or later you will want to talk about something more important. Then how can you transition smoothly to that from small talk? Work in pairs. Watch the video "Small Talk to Business Talk" and discuss with your partner about the following questions.

1.   **What did the speaker in the video clip say in order to transition to business talk?**

_____

_____

_____

2.   **What questions will you ask to transition from small talk to more important conversations?**

_____

_____

_____

3.   **If you need to transition from small talk to research related topics, what questions will you ask?**

_____

_____

_____

Task 3

One benefit of attending academic events is the prospect of making new friends in a certain field. Watch a video entitled "How Speed Networking Could Work at Your Next Conference" and complete the following exercises.

1. **Watch the video ONCE and decide what benefits of speed networking are NOT mentioned in the video?**

    A. You can meet with a wide range of people you wouldn't otherwise meet.

    B. It's highly efficient.

    C. You can make many new contacts in a short period of time.

    D. There's no need of self-introductions.

    E. The time frame allows you to converse and possibly set up a time for future meeting.

    F. You don't need to worry about the exit.

    G. If you don't connect, you can be saved by the bell.

    H. Meeting people who are related to your research is very nice.

    I. You may find people who can help you solve problems in your work.

    J. You can meet people and talk about projects and some prospects.

2. **Watch the video again and take down notes about how to do speed networking in just five minutes. Fill each blank with ONE word.**

    1) Prepare _____ second blurb about yourself.

    2) Have business cards _____.

    3) Be aware of the _____ factor.

    4) Stick to the _____ info.

    5) Take notes on the _____ of your partner's business card.

    6) Have fun and _____.

    If you cannot finish your talk within the time frame, you can:

    7) Suggest the _____ step.

    8) _____ them during a coffee break.

    9) Meet them at a poster to _____ further.

    10) Send them an _____ after the event.

Task 4

For master students, PhD students, and postdoc researchers as well, it is important to network with peers and key researchers at an academic conference. It is even vital to your success as a professional in your field. Watch the video "How to Network at an Academic Conference" and complete the following exercises.

1. **Watch the video ONCE and take down notes about the strategies to network at a conference. Based on your notes, decide when these tips should be used. Fill in the blanks with the corresponding tips.**

    1) Before the conference: _____

    2) During the conference: _____

    3) After the conference: _____

    A. Prepare conversation starters.

    B. Send them a "Thank you" message.

    C. Plan exit strategies.

    D. Repeat people's names in the interaction.

    E. Prepare elevator pitches.

    F. Make use of exhibitor booths and conference badges.

    G. Do your homework on your potential network.

    H. Organize the business cards you receive.

    I. Send them articles of interest.

    J. Make contact beforehand.

    K. Make use of idle time.

    L. Bring along your business cards.

    M. Know your limits and don't spread yourself too thin.

    N. Keep networking after the conference.

    O. Design your schedule.

    P. Maintain a "give" attitude.

2. **Watch the video again. Take down notes of the two examples of elevator pitches and think about their differences. Prepare two versions of your own elevator pitch, one for non-experts, and the other for experts in your field. Then work in pairs. Present your two versions to your partner and ask for comments.**

    A sample of a clear and concise elevator pitch:

    _____

    _____

_____

_____

A bad sample: _____

_____

The differences: _____

_____

Two versions of your own elevator pitch:

_____

_____

_____

_____

_____

_____

_____

_____

_____

_____

3. **What does the speaker mean when he says "Bring your business cards, but don't rely on them"? Exchange your ideas with your pair-work partner.**

4. **How do you understand this "give" attitude when you approach networking? Is it the same as altruism? Practice explaining it to your partner before you share your view in class.**

Task 5

When you are expanding your network at an academic event, you may have to try to enter a conversation. Then what is the appropriate way to start a conversation, or join a conversation? You may find the following talk enlightening. Watch the talk "The Best Way to Enter a Conversation at a Networking Event" and complete the following exercises.

1. **Watch the video ONCE and decide whether the statements are true (T) or false (F).**

    1) It is wise to approach people who are standing alone by complimenting them on something, such as their glasses, purse, or their outfit.　　　　(　)

2) It is rude to approach people who are standing alone by asking them about the drink they are holding.   (   )

3) A good way to walk up to a group is to interrupt them directly.   (   )

4) When you approach a group, you can just come in, listen and get an idea of the conversation. And when you can contribute, do so and introduce yourself while keeping the conversation going.   (   )

5) An easy way to join a group is to approach them and say "I'm XXX. I don't know anybody here. Can I join you?"   (   )

6) If you want to join a group, always choose the loudest group because they are having the greatest fun and you don't want to miss it.   (   )

2.   **Work in a group of four. Discuss the following questions with your group members: Are the speaker's tips convincing and worth trying? Why or why not? Then share your ideas with the whole class.**

📖 Project

Suppose you have just been accepted as a presenter of your research in an academic conference in a few months. Besides making preparation about your presentation, you can also prepare for your networking. Work in groups and go over this unit together. Make a list of things you need to prepare, such as a name list of people you need to contact, conversation starters, elevator pitches, business cards, your resume, and formal clothes. You can make a presentation in class about the preparations you have made. Compare your preparations with those of other groups with regards to the focus of preparation, and how detailed the preparation is for each aspect.

教师服务

感谢您选用清华大学出版社的教材！为了更好地服务教学，我们为授课教师提供本学科重点教材信息及样书，请您扫码获取。

▶▶ 最新书目

扫码获取 2024 **外语类**重点教材信息

▶▶ 样书赠送

教师扫码即可获取样书